Ghosts, Smoke, and the Badge

Ghosts, Smoke, and the Badge

A MEMOIR OF BROTHERHOOD, FEAR, AND THE WEIGHT OF DUTY

DR. DONDI M. DAY

With a Foreword by Capt. Dan Willis (Ret.)
Author of *Bulletproof Spirit*

Introduction by Dr. Travis Yates
Author of *The Courageous Police Leader*

Copyright and Disclaimer

Library of Congress Control Number: Pending

ISBN: 979-8-218-89329-3

Publisher:
Dondi M. Day

P.O. Box 5041
Emerald Isle, NC 28594-5041

Disclaimer / A Note to Readers and Educators

This book is a work of literary nonfiction based on true events. To protect privacy and prevent misidentification, certain names, dates, locations, and identifying details have been changed or combined. Some characters are composites, and select events have been adapted or condensed for narrative clarity. Any resemblance to actual persons, living or deceased, or to specific incidents is coincidental.

This book draws on lived experience rather than formal research while reflecting themes commonly explored in leadership, ethics, and organizational behavior. The stories presented here are not offered as prescriptions or instruction but as lived moments meant to invite reflection, conversation, and judgment rather than easy conclusions.

Readers may find value in approaching these chapters as narrative case studies that raise questions of responsibility, restraint, moral injury, leadership under pressure, and the quiet costs of service. While rooted in law enforcement, the themes explored extend beyond any single profession and may be useful in leadership development, ethics courses, or professional training settings that emphasize character, decision-making, and accountability.

Dedication

To God—for every step I survived, every lesson I learned, and every ounce of strength that was never mine alone.

To Chief Steve Lewis (Ret.), whose leadership shaped not only the officer I became but also the man I carried forward long after the job.

To Sgt. Sean Pearson (Ret.), for showing me how to dance when the weight grew heavy, and for the kind of wisdom that reminds us life keeps moving, even after the sirens fade.

To John Styron (Ret.), a dispatcher whose steady voice cut through the noise and guided us when clarity mattered most.

In memory of Sgt. Lenton T. Lewis (Ret., USCG BMC) and Sgt. Micah S. O'Neal (USMC PFC), Vietnam veterans whose service and example endure beyond uniform and time.

And in memory of Chief Marvin P. Knox (Ret., USMC GySgt; Ret. Chief of Police), a veteran of the Korean War and two tours in Vietnam, whose leadership carried forward long after the uniforms came off.

This is for you, with gratitude deeper than these pages can hold.

And finally, to my family:

To my wife, Tracey—the anchor in every storm and the steady light in every dark season. You carried burdens no one else could see, and your strength made it possible for me to keep showing up. Your patience, grace, and quiet courage are woven into every page of this book.

To my sons, Brayden and Logan—you grew up with a father who chased sirens and missed holidays and birthdays, yet you never stopped believing in me. You reminded me that the badge is temporary, but fatherhood is forever. You are, and always will be, my proudest legacy.

Table of Contents

Foreword—Capt. Dan Willis (Ret.)

When Dr. Dondi Day—a former police officer with more than two decades of service—first asked me to review his personal memoir, *Ghosts, Smoke, and the Badge*, and consider writing a foreword, I was intrigued. After reading it, I was honored—and impressed beyond words.

This is an unforgettable memoir of what it truly means to serve. It is real, powerful, and deeply human. Reading it stirred memories—experiences long forgotten, buried, or misunderstood—and gave renewed meaning to moments that have shaped not only my own career but also the lives of everyone who has ever worn a badge.

Whether you are in law enforcement, another first responder profession, a loved one of someone who serves, or simply a reader drawn to true stories of courage, resilience, and brotherhood, *Ghosts, Smoke, and the Badge* offers a compelling portrait of a life lived in service. It captures what it means to answer an inner calling to protect life—and to love those who do.

This is a poetic, beautifully written memoir that reveals the human side of policing: the quiet burdens, small victories, brotherhood, trauma, and emotional weight most people never see—and that first responders themselves rarely have the space to fully understand. It is the job as Dr. Day lived it: sometimes funny, sometimes terrifying, often humbling, yet always honest. With more than forty years in the profession, I can say without hesitation that I have never read a more authentic or personal account—one that moved me profoundly.

Dr. Day reminds us that first responders are human beings—real people who fear, bleed, and suffer like everyone else. What separates them is not invincibility, but courage born from a deep desire to be good amid the bad. They choose to look beyond danger and personal pain for the opportunity to protect and help others. In that choice, they find purpose.

In a profession that can feel darker than the eternal black of death itself, we find our way forward through the light left by those who came before us. Dr. Day demystifies service, inviting readers into the brotherhood that sustains and heals the heartaches, the adventure, and the ghosts of moments that linger for a lifetime. Every call becomes a thread in the fabric of who we are becoming. How we respond—whether with intention or avoidance—will either strengthen that fabric or tear it apart.

Dr. Day writes eloquently about the brotherhood shared across all first responder professions. We are united not only by trauma but also by love for the work—and for one another. We all carry unseen weight from the responsibility of the badge, which at times can feel like a lead anchor. Yet through that same badge, we also experience moments of grace—an almost angelic touch that reminds us why we serve. He emphasizes the importance of keeping life's priorities aligned with what gives life to the heart and meaning to the soul.

This book gives voice to a truth many first responders live but struggle to name: this profession is an ongoing process of transformation—learning to recover, heal, overcome, and love even through heartache. As Dr. Day writes, "The worst moments still have pieces of grace in them." Focusing on those moments—on brotherhood, shared experience, and love—keeps us from disappearing into the relentless noise and darkness of a profession we deeply cherish.

This is not an instructional manual. It is a memoir—story-driven and reflective—that allows the reader to feel the realities of service rather than be told about them. Through lived experience, Dr. Day shows how to remain human amid hardship, tracing a journey from living inside a relentless storm to discovering what lies beyond the badge: the enduring essence of who we are and our capacity to love and do good.

Dr. Day's message is ultimately uplifting. Even in the hardest moments, strength is found in one another and in shared service calling that, when carried with honor, profoundly shapes a life.

This is an important and timely book, especially in an era of unprecedented challenges facing law enforcement and all first responder professions. It offers insight, understanding, inspiration, and—most importantly—hope. I strongly encourage you to take this book to heart. It will deepen your awareness, move you, challenge you, and empower you.

Capt. Dan Willis (Ret.)
Author of *Bulletproof Spirit*
firstresponderwellness.com

Introduction—Dr. Travis Yates

I've read more than my share of memoirs written by those who wore the badge, and frankly, I'm rarely impressed by war stories. Too many are thinly veiled therapy sessions, while others read like exercises in ego—less about insight and more about being seen. Most will come and go, lost in the next wave of look-at-me confessions, remembered briefly and then forgotten entirely.

This is not that book.

The ending words of Dr. Dondi Day's *Ghosts, Smoke, and the Badge* should have told me that: "This is my story, but it's also our story."

At the turn of each page, I found myself seeing myself—the first call, the mentors, the legends that came before us. The calls that never really ended. The dreams in the middle of the night you wouldn't wish on anyone.

Like Dr. Day, it took me decades to understand the profession I had inherited, and that is the real value of the book you hold in your hands. If you are looking backward, it offers peace in knowing you are not alone. If you are looking forward, it challenges you to see the profession not as it was handed to you, but as it must be carried.

This is not for the faint of heart. You may be reading stories from one career law enforcement professional, but you are in the plot—and that storyline is both painful and rewarding. Let me encourage you to give in and allow your mind to go to the very places you want to forget.

Embrace the ghosts and walk through the smoke. This is how the profession is understood—and this is how it endures.

Dr. Travis Yates

Author of *The Courageous Police Leader*

TravisYates.org

Oath of Office—State of North Carolina

I, _____, do solemnly swear (or affirm) that I will support the Constitution of the United States; that I will be faithful and bear true allegiance to the State of North Carolina and to the constitutional powers and authorities that are, or may be, established for the government thereof; and that I will endeavor to support, maintain, and defend the Constitution of said State, not inconsistent with the Constitution of the United States, to the best of my knowledge and ability.

I further swear (or affirm) that I will faithfully, impartially, and honestly discharge the duties of my office as a law-enforcement officer; that I will be vigilant in enforcing the laws of this State and the ordinances of the jurisdiction I serve; that I will not allow personal feelings, prejudice, animosity, or friendship to influence my decisions; and that I will conduct myself with integrity, courage, and respect for human life and dignity.

So help me God.

Chapter 1—Running Toward the Noise

A cop is shaped in the moments they choose to move
toward what others turn away from.

—Author's Reflection

The night of my first chase didn't begin with chaos—it began with the feeling that something in the air was changing. A shift you sensed, like a cool wind brushing your face.

When the moment finally arrives—the movement, the adrenaline, the radio shattering the quiet—you know everything has changed.

I didn't have the experience then to understand what that feeling meant. I only knew the streets suddenly felt as if they were holding their breath. That kind of tension means something is moving toward you, something about to break.

Some nights deliver the truth about this job fast and snap your senses alive. They show how quickly the ordinary can collapse into chaos. Moments like that don't appear from nowhere; they collide with the parts of you already built—instinct, fear, and whatever calm you've managed to carry.

After the chase, the van was wrecked and burning.

Years later, I can still smell the smoke. I sense the way a quiet night can tip without warning, boredom collapsing into fire.

Standing in the haze of a wrecked van, metal popping in the slow burn, I learned that courage isn't the absence of fear—it's the decision to move toward it.

Only later did I understand that night wasn't an ending or a beginning. It was something deeper pushing to the surface: instinct. An inner compass stirring long before a badge ever touched my chest. The job didn't create it; it simply shook it awake.

Even now, I recognize that same force in movies—crowds parting, officers running toward danger with purpose. A moment before motion, when something inside says go.

But that instinct doesn't begin with training or tactics. It starts earlier. For me, it started at home.

* * *

I grew up watching people step into danger with calm resolve. Even when it cost them more than anyone realized, they carried it without complaint. Their strength lived in the corners of our house—in the photos on the walls, in the pauses in my mother's voice.

Those moments became anchors. Silent ghosts that stayed with me long after childhood faded.

I stepped into policing believing I'd chosen the path myself. The older I get, the more I see it differently. Some roads feel chosen; others feel inherited.

Now I believe I was placed on it.

And the moments that shape you rarely announce themselves. They begin quietly, unremarkable, carrying a shift you don't recognize until it's too late to turn back.

I didn't know it then, but the first time the job showed me its teeth would come without drama or warning.

It would arrive on a winter night, dressed up as boredom.

Boredom into Terror

It was one of those winter nights when the town seemed to have gone to sleep without me. The air was sharp enough to sting my lungs. The streets stretched empty, the cruiser humming through the frozen town. Hours like that dragged—slow and heavy—until you wondered if police work was little more than paperwork and stale coffee.

Somewhere beyond the waterfront, the old Victorian houses along Front Street stood dark and still, their porches and peaked roofs lined up like witnesses. You couldn't hear the water lapping against the docks from the inland roads, but the silence felt held, like the town was waiting.

Nights like that made you believe the shift would stay calm, that nothing waited beyond the next curve. The job has a way of turning calm into something deceptive—a reminder that silence is never just silence.

The radio stayed dead for so long I keyed the mic once, just to hear the repeater click. I'd forgotten the volume was wide open, and the first crackle crashed through the cruiser hard enough to jolt me out of my skin.

"Unit 819, respond. Suspicious vehicle, convenience store."

Not a store—just a row of vending machines humming under a dying yellow lamp.

I rolled in as a white van pulled away—slow, deliberate, like innocence rehearsed. I eased in behind it, already running through the stop in my head as my hand reached for the mic.

Before I could run the tag, the back doors flew open.

A man leaned out, shotgun leveled at my windshield.

For a second, the world narrowed to the barrel and the thin seam of glass between us. I leaned across the console and keyed the mic.

"Gun!"

One breath.

No blast.

Instead, he started throwing newspaper boxes into the road. Heavy metal slammed against asphalt and erupted into a spray of loose quarters. Coins spun wild in the headlights, bright as sparks off steel.

I swerved, but not fast enough. The cruiser clipped one box, the impact shuddering through the frame. Sparks scattered in an orange arc as the box skidded under my bumper and tumbled into the ditch.

Instinct took over. I hit the lights, let the siren tear open the night, and felt the engine surge. The van weaved down dark county roads, its taillights cutting through the pine shadows. The smell of hot rubber and scorched brakes filled the cabin, metallic and bitter on the back of my tongue. Windblown sand rattled against the windshield like Velcro ripping apart.

My pulse thundered in my ears, loud enough to drown out the engine. Smoke trailed from the van, carrying that burnt-transmission tang that clings to you long after the danger passes.

The sergeant's voice cut through the static—calm, clipped, and steady.

"819, give speed and location every minute. Stay in it, but stay smart."

A beat later, lower but firm:

"Backup's out of position, but they're en route. Dispatch, set the tones off and notify the next county."

I answered, my voice tighter than I wanted.

One curve ahead.

They never made it.

The van plowed into the ditch, metal screeching, glass scattering across the blacktop. Steam curled into the cold night air. Backup slid in behind me, and together we pulled the suspects from the wrecked vehicle.

*   *   *

When it was over, the stillness hit harder than the chase. It wasn't calm. It felt hollow, like the air hadn't decided if the danger was done. Your pulse doesn't settle right away. It argues with your mind long after the threat is gone. Outside, the night held its silence—no wind, no sirens, nothing but the world catching its breath.

I remember standing there as the wrecker winched the mangled van upright. My hands shook, so I shoved them in my pockets. The smells lingered in the cold air.

Some nights stay with you whether you want them to or not.

*   *   *

Somewhere beyond the wreck, I knew the town was untouched by what had just happened on the road. Mist drifted through the blue lights as the quiet settled back in—heavier now, older somehow.

That was the rhythm of the job: stillness stretched thin over chaos. You never knew when it would crack or how long the lull would last before it did.

The hush that followed never really left me. It lived beneath every shift that came after—the radio static, the laughter, the routine calls with their hidden edges. That night was my first real taste of what I'd stepped into. Fear, control, duty, and whatever faith God had already placed in me were being tested.

Years later, I understood that night wasn't about the chase. It was about learning how to live in what comes after. The job has a way of teaching lessons like that—slow at first, then all at once—until you start tracing the line back to where it really began.

For me, that line didn't start with a radio call. It started long before training and shift work began shaping who I was becoming—before rookie school, before my first solo shift, before blue lights ever reflected off a windshield.

Every story has a beginning. Mine started before I was born—etched into family photographs and folded uniforms. Some people inherit land or money. I inherited a calling that smelled like leather and gun oil. Its weight was displayed in picture frames long before it ever rested on my chest.

The Rhythm of Inheritance

To understand the instinct that steadied me that night, you have to know the roots it came from. In our family, the uniform was more than a job—it was an inheritance. My grandfather wore the badge before any of us, and his death still ripples through our bloodline, an ache that never fully goes away. He was one of the patients murdered by Donald Harvey, the hospital orderly who called himself the Angel of Death while poisoning the people he was sworn to help. Harvey claimed mercy; what he delivered was betrayal. My grandfather's death became our reminder of how fragile trust can be, even in the hands meant to protect or heal.

In families like ours, the past doesn't fade; it settles into the corners of your life. It lingers in stories, photographs, and the things people choose not to say. Those memories lean forward into who we become, shaping us long after the moments themselves have passed.

There's an old photograph of him at my mother's house, its edges gone soft, the color washed into pale gold. He's standing beside his cruiser, hat cocked slightly, calm but alert. As a kid, I studied that photo for long stretches, trying to understand what he saw when the camera clicked—what he already knew about duty, danger, or the thin space between them. His eyes held the stillness I'd later recognize in veteran officers: calm shaped by surviving what others never see.

My father followed, first into the Marine Corps and later into local law enforcement. His time in uniform didn't last long. Maybe it was what he carried home from overseas, or burdens that held on tighter than he did. When I was older, I asked why he quit. We were standing in the kitchen, rain ticking against the window, when he looked outside and said, "It changes you." His shoulders sagged as if the words themselves carried weight—a kind of exhaustion etched far beneath anything he could explain.

My younger brother stepped into the job too. I pinned the badge on his chest the day he graduated from the academy, my hand steady even though I knew what waited once the applause faded. My mother clapped with everyone else, but her smile faltered when the flash went off. Pride and fear lived side by side on her face, and she prayed for us more than we ever prayed for ourselves.

The Coast Guard taught me discipline before the streets ever could. At sea, control wasn't theory—it was survival. Some nights I stood watch on deck, wind cutting across my face, the Atlantic stretching out—endless and indifferent. Out there, readiness became its own form of faith, a steadiness that followed me from the cutter to rookie school and eventually to the driver's seat of a patrol car.

I grew up in a small coastal town where the air stayed thick with humidity and the ocean was never far from earshot. Everyone knew your family name; legacy carried its own kind of weight. Some of the older deputies remembered my grandfather and would nod when they heard my last name. It wasn't judgment—it was a question: Would I rise to the standard or fall short of it?

People still ask why anyone runs toward chaos. There isn't one reason. For some, it's duty; for others, faith. For me, it wasn't heroism—it was a reflex wired deep. You learn to crave it more than comfort. There's a rush in holding the thin space between chaos and order, even if no one says it out loud.

When you're young, you think adrenaline will carry you. Later, you learn it's breath—the steady rhythm that lets you move when everything around you starts to break apart. The badge didn't give me fearlessness; it gave me focus. And that focus is what lets you step toward the noise—the fear, the motion, the split second where everything demands a decision—instead of freezing inside it.

Rookie school would take that raw instinct and carve it into skill. The classroom, the drills, the field exercises—all of it waited ahead, ready to turn instinct into something I could trust when the real noise began.

Rookie School

The academy was where that instinct began to take shape. It wasn't a classroom; it was controlled chaos. We were a mix—veterans chasing purpose, single parents searching for stability, and kids too young to understand what they were stepping into. Different stories, same crucible. Our courage would be measured by how steady we stood alone, how well we carried each other, and how we kept moving forward when everything instilled in us wanted to stop.

Day one felt like shock therapy. The dressing room smelled of soap, sweat, and cleaning solution. Someone muttered something about last rites; no one laughed. By noon we were soaked through, half of us convinced we'd made the worst decision of our lives. By week two, those same people were cheering each other through runs that would've dropped us flat days earlier.

Mornings started before dawn. Cold air. Fogged breath. Instructors moved down the rows like wolves hunting weakness. Push-ups until arms failed. Miles until the horizon blurred. They weren't testing muscle; they were testing surrender—how far you'd bend before you broke. The ones who stayed learned to take the pain and center themselves when no one else could.

The humor was dark and exhausted—the kind that bubbles up when quitting feels easier. We gave each other nicknames. One recruit locked his knees during inspection and toppled like a tree. "Timber," from then on. We laughed because laughter kept us upright. We didn't know it yet, but those stupid jokes were the first threads of a bond that would matter far more later.

Inside the classroom, the pain changed shape. Statutes, case law, and policy binders that smelled like ink and plastic. We memorized Miranda until it lived in our dreams. The track built endurance. The classroom built precision—the ability to think while your pulse tried to drown every thought.

Then the instructors shifted gears. Muscle and memory were one thing—now they wanted to know what we'd do when consequence entered the room. Firearms Week began. I thought I understood guns. The Coast Guard had trained me well enough, but the day the instructor placed a chrome-plated .357 in my hands, I felt weight in a new way. Heavier than it looked—cold, unforgiving, balanced between power and consequence. Hollywood lied. There was no glory here—just gravity.

The revolver barked thunder and flame. Smoke curled around us. Hot brass from the semi-autos scattered across the gravel—or down your collar if you were unlucky. No flinching. You learned to take the pain. The smell of burnt powder clung to everything, an aroma every officer recognizes long after their academy days are gone.

Even on the range, the noise wasn't just the gunfire—it was the adrenaline, the recoil, the doubt, and the pressure to get it right. Firearms week wasn't really about accuracy. It was about mastering the noise—every distraction, every spike of fear, every thought trying to pull your attention off the front sight. Master it, or it masters you.

Accuracy wasn't the hardest test. Judgment was.

A man reaching into his waistband.

A woman clutching something shiny.

One blink to decide—one breath to steady your shot.

Shoot or don't.

I got it wrong more than once—fired when I shouldn't have, hesitated when I couldn't afford to. Each mistake was replayed on the big screen while the class watched in silence. Humiliation became its own instructor. It always worked.

Stress shoots came next—sprint until your lungs burned, then fire; shout commands until your voice cracked, then fire again. The instructor stalked behind us with a loudhailer, barking contradictions over the wail of sirens while blue lights strobed across the range. Targets blurred at the edges, sweat stung your eyes, and your pulse hammered against the trigger guard. The paper didn't matter—control did. If you could steady your breath while your heart tried to escape your chest, you might survive the real thing.

Then came judgment drills—scenarios that cut closer than any paper silhouette.

A man shifting his weight.

A glint of metal.

A teenager reaching into his pocket.

The teenager scenario stayed with me. He reached into his pocket, and for half a breath I saw headlines forming around my name—lawsuits, vigils, and a mother's face I'd never forget. My lungs stopped working. Then the object appeared—a pack of gum. My trigger finger froze. That night I lay awake replaying the moment until the ceiling felt as heavy as the gun on my nightstand.

Training forces you into the space where fear crowds out clarity. And afterward, the question is always the same: Would I get it right when it counted?

Then the academy reminded us that the job wasn't just about force—it was about saving lives. CPR until our arms trembled. Tourniquets until our fingers cramped. Crash scenes staged with fake blood that smelled far too close to real. I remember kneeling beside a volunteer "victim," hands shaking so badly I almost dropped the airway kit. Even knowing it was practice, some part of me believed fumbling would cost someone their life. In the real world, hesitation kills as surely as any weapon.

Some scenarios tested restraint instead of reaction—a homeless man asleep on a bench, a teenager threatening herself, a domestic argument that was really a plea for help. The hardest weapon to master was your own voice. And always, teamwork. In one drill, I was pinned against a wall until my partner crashed in to help. The instructor didn't raise his voice. He just nodded and said, "That's why you never do this alone." He was right. Out there, ego kills; trust saves.

Late in the afternoon, we'd gather in the hallway outside the training rooms, eating vending-machine chips under humming fluorescent lights, swapping stories about what scared us most. Fear came out sideways—through sarcasm, cheap jokes, and forced laughter. We called it emotional camouflage.

By graduation week, the badge no longer felt like a symbol. It felt earned. The metal they pinned on us wasn't honor—it was responsibility made tangible, a weight I felt even before it rested against my chest.

Graduation

Graduation came faster than anyone expected. One morning we were gasping through a five-mile run; the next we were standing in pressed uniforms, faces still marked with disbelief that we'd made it through. Families filled the bleachers. Cameras flashed like lightning, each burst cutting through a current of pride. The room smelled of starch, shoe polish, and the gravity of what came next.

When they called my name, I stepped forward. My Chief pinned the badge on my chest, and for the first time it felt heavy for the right reasons. The speeches blurred together—honor, service, courage, and sacrifice. There wasn't any profound stillness. No cinematic moment. Just a weight against my chest and the quiet understanding that whatever happened next would test whether I deserved to wear it.

My younger brother clapped me on the shoulder and said, "Now it's real." Then he gave me that half-grin—the one that meant the joke was coming—and added, "You sure you got what it takes?" Brothers speak in jabs, not compliments. Cops do too, I would learn. I smiled, though my stomach was still somewhere between the ceremony and the street. My mother hugged me longer than usual, whispering something about staying safe, as if safety were still a choice.

We were no longer students. We stood on the thin edge before experience, about to learn who we were when it counted.

Outside, the gym doors gave way to a gray sky. Rain had started to fall—thin, cold, and steady. It soaked into the fabric of my uniform, dulling the shine of new cloth, grounding me. The rain cooled the adrenaline. It reminded me that the job cared nothing for ceremonies. Patrol cars lined the curb, their antennas bending slightly in the wind. For a moment, I just listened. The radios inside crackled softly with static, faint voices breaking in and out. I realized one of those voices would soon be mine.

That night, when the uniform hung damp in my closet, the memory of graduation already felt distant. The next test wouldn't be in a gym. It would be on the street.

The gym applause faded, and the job wasted no time reminding me it had its own way of welcoming rookies. Every squad has its own initiation—some harsh, some hilarious. Mine came wrapped in fog and laughter.

Statues of Broken Wings

It started with a simple call. I was in the squad bay killing time—busywork, forms, anything to look useful while waiting to get assigned to a permanent shift. The room buzzed with low chatter and the hum of old fluorescent lights. I was double-checking a stack of patrol logs when my corporal stepped into the doorway, leaning on the frame with a look I hadn't learned to read yet.

"We've had reports of a figure wandering the old cemetery off of Ann Street," he said, professional and measured.

I was new, still polishing the shine off my badge.

The cemetery—the Old Burying Ground—sat in the historic district where the pavement narrowed and the oak trees leaned in. Deeded to the town in the early 1700s, it felt older than any line on a map. Stone walls sagged with age. Names weathered away by decades of rain.

The wrought-iron gates moaned as we forced them open, hinges protesting like something half-alive. The metal burned cold beneath my palm. Fog rose off the creek and slid across the path, curling around the headstones as if it had been waiting for us.

I remember thinking how quiet it was—not peaceful, just hollow. The kind of quiet that presses back when you step into it.

My flashlight pushed through the mist and caught on the broken wings of statues scattered along the path. Sound sharpened—the grind of gravel, the thud of my steps, the breath I couldn't silence. Every noise came back at me, as if the whole place were listening.

The corporal nodded toward the fence line. "Take the right side," he said. "Meet you in the middle."

I read the names on the stones out loud to steady myself—old family names I'd seen in school. In the fog, even they sounded unfamiliar.

The air tasted like limestone and wet leaves. Somewhere a branch snapped—too sharp, too close. Another rustle off to the left. My hand went to my holster.

"Show yourself!" I said, trying to sound calm and not quite making it.

Two shapes exploded from behind a row of headstones, howling with laughter so hard one of them nearly toppled into a grave. My "suspect" and my corporal could barely stand. One wiped the tears from his eyes, gasping something about "rookies."

I didn't laugh at first. My pulse pounded, fingers numb from squeezing the grip of my weapon. When it finally settled, I let out a shaky breath and grinned. They'd sent the rookie to chase ghosts, and I'd walked through that fog—afraid but steady.

Weeks later, someone at roll call started humming the Ghostbusters theme. Everyone cracked up, including me. The nickname stuck—half joke, half reminder. The haze, the stone angels, the way my boots kept moving even when instinct screamed to turn back—it all settled into one truth: fear never disappears; you just learn how to walk with it.

After my shift that night, I drove past the cemetery again. The fog had lifted, and dawn pushed a thin light across the stones. Nothing moved. No shadows. No tricks. Just a quiet place on an ordinary street.

They called it a prank.

I called it a lesson.

Courage isn't loud.

Sometimes it's just the sound of your own boots moving forward in the dark.

The Precipice of Becoming

Some lessons don't come from classrooms or manuals. They arrive in the heat of a single day—in the faces of strangers who've just lost the illusion that the world is safe. Every officer remembers the first call that strips away the last thin layer of certainty and leaves something steadier behind.

I had the uniform and the training, but not a place to land yet—just riding with whoever had an empty seat while I waited to be assigned a field training officer. The same corporal who'd once sent me ghost-hunting through a fog-choked cemetery let me ride with him in the meantime. My uniform was still crisp, my belt stiff, and the shine on my badge almost too bright. Rookies went where there was room, learning from whoever happened to be behind the wheel.

When dispatch cracked through the radio—"Man with a gun, housing complex off Seaside Court. Multiple callers"—my pulse jumped before I did. The corporal jerked his chin toward the cruiser.

"Get in."

Siren on. Lights flashing. The town blurred past in sunlit fragments— storefronts, crosswalks, and heat shimmering on the windshield. We shot past the old hardware store on Highway 70, the boarded-up fish market, everything sliding by like scenery borrowed from someone else's life.

Seaside Court sat low and tired near the marsh—two-story units sagging under the weight of years. Kids' bikes leaned against chain-link fences. A fryer vent pushed out the smell of old grease. It looked harmless until it didn't.

When I stepped out of the cruiser, the air tightened. Curtains flicked. A door slammed somewhere deep in the maze of buildings. Tension pooled fast—restless and waiting.

Dispatch fed us fragments. "Male, late twenties. Dark shirt. Waving a handgun near Building C." No one knew where he'd gone, and that uncertainty carried its own gravity.

The corporal hung back, letting me feel the scene before he shaped it. The same quiet test as the cemetery—only this one wouldn't end in laughter.

A child stood near the breezeway—barefoot, clutching a teddy bear. She wasn't crying. Just frozen in the hush that follows panic.

"Go inside," I said. My voice sounded steadier than I felt.

Her mother rushed forward, scooped her up, and scanned the lot with wide, searching eyes.

Every parked car felt like a blind corner. Every shadow threatened to become something worse. We moved between buildings the way the academy drilled us—angles, cover, thin slices of sunlight and dark—waiting for the flash of steel or the wrong movement that changed everything.

Backup units rolled in. Voices overlapped through the static. We cleared stairwells, breezeways, and laundry rooms. Each resident told a different version of the same fear.

By midafternoon, the man had vanished—into the neighborhood, into the marsh, into rumor.

The danger faded. The adrenaline didn't. It clung beneath the skin, humming long after the scene was safe.

* * *

When it finally drained, it left a faint after-tremor. The little girl sat wrapped in a blanket, teddy bear tucked beneath her chin. Her mother whispered something about moving. Fear makes a family pack long before the boxes appear.

Back in the cruiser, my hands were still trembling. The corporal glanced over.

"Not bad," he said. "You moved when it counted."

No smile. No ceremony. Just a quiet acknowledgment that landed harder than applause ever could.

We cleared Seaside Court and stopped for gas. The sun was still high, bleaching the day into something flat and unreal. For the first time, I wondered if maybe I did belong out there—right as the radio reminded me the job doesn't care what you've already faced.

Where Grace Shows Up

"Assist Fire Department with structure fire. Residential. Two-story. Smoke visible."

It sounded simple. Calls like that usually do.

But as we turned down the street, a column of black smoke lifted above the rooftops, visible nearly a mile out. Flames punched through the siding, sharp and determined. Heat rolled across the asphalt and hammered against the cruiser's windshield.

Neighbors clustered barefoot in their yards, one hand shading their faces, the other holding phones. A football game blared from a TV across the street—the sound of normal life running beside disaster.

On the curb sat a family of four—mother, father, and two kids—wrapped in thin blankets. The father's forearms were raw and blistered. He kept wringing his hands like he could pull the moment back.

A firefighter, steam lifting off his turnout gear, gave me the shorthand.

"Charcoal grill on the deck. A few coals fell through the boards. He stepped inside to check the game—by the time he smelled it, the siding was already lit."

Too late. The house was gone.

The father's voice was rough but steady.

"We lost everything," he said. "But we're safe. The house can be rebuilt."
He looked at his family. "That's what matters."

Behind him, firefighters worked with quiet precision. Water met the flames with a sharp hiss, steam lifting like breath from the street. Sunlight caught the spray and turned it into a trembling rainbow.

When the last flame died, a heavier calm settled over the street. Smoke drifted low, reluctant to leave. The smell clung to my uniform, my skin, and the cruiser's seats.

You see many kinds of loss in this job—but sometimes it's just a spark that gets away from you. One distraction. One moment. And everything becomes heat and memory.

That man had it right, though. He still had what mattered.

* * *

Before shift change, we stopped at the firehouse to grab some bad coffee. The bay doors were open, trucks gleaming under the harsh lights. The air smelled of burnt wiring and damp gear—heavy, lived-in, earned.

The firefighter who'd given me the rundown sat at a table, elbows on his knees, soot smudged across his face. His jacket hung over the back of his chair, reflective stripes catching the fluorescent light in tired pulses. When he leaned forward, a small silver cross slipped out from beneath his T-shirt—a little tarnished, shaped by years of being held onto more than shown.

"You're the one who answered that gun call?" he asked.

"Yeah," I said.

He let out a laugh that sounded more like fatigue than humor.

"You run into gunfire."

I shrugged. "You run into fires."

A slow grin worked across his face. "Guess neither of us gets paid enough to be normal."

He turned his mug in slow circles, ceramic ticking softly against the metal tabletop. His gaze drifted—some collapsing hallway of smoke I'd never see. His jaw set for half a second, the way a man braces for something only he can feel. Then he blinked it off and came back to the room. The vending machine hummed in the corner. Sirens wailed faintly outside, and we both turned instinctively toward the sound.

Different jobs. Same muscle memory.

"Long day," he said.

"It's been something," I answered.

He nodded, fumbling his gear. "A family lost a house today. But they made it out. That's a win, even if it doesn't look like one."

I thought of the father on the curb. Of the little girl at Seaside Court clutching her teddy bear.

"It's strange," I said, "how the worst moments still have pieces of grace in them."

He nodded once. "That's what keeps us showing up," he said, thumb brushing the small cross at his collar. "Grace shows up in places we don't."

Outside, the coastal sky faded from gold to gray—the twilight that makes you wonder how one shift can hold so much life, loss, and everything in between. The whole exchange was just a handful of words, but it stayed with me.

*　*　*

By the end of that day, I'd learned something the academy never mentioned. Every call leaves a trace—the smoke you smell after a shower, the quiet stare of a child under a streetlight.

Loss spreads like fire—quiet at first, just a spark—until it shows you what's left when safety burns away.

By the next afternoon, something in me had settled. Not confidence—just awareness. The kind that comes after a few hard calls, when the job stops feeling theoretical and starts showing its edges. And that was when the assignment list went up in the squad room—the moment the drifting stopped and the real shaping began.

I'd seen how fast a day could strip you down—fear in one call, grace in the next, loss woven through both. What I needed now was someone who knew how to stand inside all of it.

*   *   *

In the station, rookies talked about a veteran officer everyone seemed to know without really knowing. I hadn't met him yet, but his name moved on its own. Some stories were about his patience. Others about his silence. They said he could settle a fight with one look—and that he'd never raised his voice on a call.

Every squad room has one name spoken with a different kind of gravity. He carried it. You'd hear his voice when things were sliding sideways—the kind of calm that steadied other units without drawing attention to itself. No swagger. No drama. Just presence.

Rookies traded stories about field training officers the way kids trade baseball cards. Some FTOs were screamers, convinced humiliation was a teaching tool. Others coasted and let rookies drift into danger. But when his name came up, the tone shifted. The jokes stopped. People spoke plainly.

"He won't yell," someone said over burnt coffee. "He'll just let you fail in front of him. That's worse."

Another officer added, "He'll let you walk right to the edge of a mistake, then stop you with one question. And you won't forget it."

I'd see him sometimes in passing—before he was anything more than a rumor—leaning against a cruiser, arms loosely crossed, posture unforced but alert. Not the tallest. Not the loudest. Just steady, like the job fit him the way a well-worn jacket does—broken in all the right places. Sometimes a dry joke slipped out before his face reset into that quiet readiness.

He carried himself like someone who didn't need to prove what he already knew.

One afternoon, I walked into the squad room and found officers gathered around the whiteboard. A new list hung there—assignments, partners, and for a few of us, our field training officers. My eyes moved down column after column, pulse ticking harder with each line.

"Who'd you get?" someone asked.

I wasn't sure yet. I read slower. Then I saw it—my name printed neatly beside his.

No nickname. No legend. Just a name.

The room narrowed for a beat. Someone behind me gave a low whistle.

"Lucky," a voice murmured. "Or unlucky. Depends on how honest you can handle someone being."

I didn't know how to feel. Part of me wanted an easy ride—someone who'd check the boxes and let me coast through my first nights. But another part—the part shaped by the man with the gun, the fire, and the child with the teddy bear—wanted the opposite. Someone who would tell me the truth before the job did it the hard way.

The older guys said he'd been through everything—bar fights, domestics gone sideways, pursuits that ended as cautionary tales. Yet when they talked about him, there was only respect. Nothing inflated. Nothing performative.

"He won't just train you," a sergeant said, flipping through paperwork. "He'll decide whether the rest of us can trust you."

I kept thinking about the little girl at Seaside Court clutching her teddy bear. The father watching his home burn. The firefighter's cross catching the light. All the quiet moments that had already begun reshaping me.

The academy taught tactics, statutes, and the mechanics of staying alive. It didn't teach you how to stand with someone whose life had just split open—or how to leave without taking their grief with you.

I had manuals. I had training. What I didn't yet have was the person who could show me how to survive contact with real nights and real people.

Soon enough, I'd meet him in the station parking lot—one FTO among several, all studying the rookies. But even before that, I knew this was the moment where drifting ended—and accountability began.

Chapter 2—Ghosts, Smoke, and What the Street Demands

Difficulties strengthen the mind, as labor does the body.

—Seneca

Some chapters of your life don't announce themselves with sirens or gunfire. They begin quietly, in the space between who you were and who you're about to become. Graduation had handed me a badge and a ceremony, but what waited afterward was something different—an unspoken test that separated rookies who only wore the uniform from the ones who learned to carry it. The traces of my training rode with me into that next chapter, but so did a simple truth: the street wasn't impressed by potential. It demanded proof.

The transition felt less like stepping into darkness and more like entering a place where instinct moved before eyesight. The academy had hardened our bodies and humbled our pride, but it hadn't yet confronted us with the reality of long nights and real consequences. I still carried the imprint of those first tests—the drills, the firing range, the baton training—lessons that sharpened my edges but hadn't yet tested my center. Those moments had opened the door, but the real learning waited beyond it. The next lesson wouldn't come from chaos. It would come from someone who knew how to move through it without letting it steer him.

Every department has a figure whose presence arrives before he does—a steady influence you sense long before you understand it. And the street, which tests every new officer in its own time, was already making room for the man who would teach me how to carry the badge.

The One Who Walked Out of the Smoke

Before I ever saw him, I felt a change ripple across the parking lot—a shift that made rookies straighten their backs without thinking. Several field training officers stood waiting for us, clipboards in hand, each with their own way of measuring the rookies who would soon ride beside them. But one of them carried a steadiness that moved through the line before he even spoke.

The veterans called him "Top." When others heard the name, their posture tightened—nothing dramatic, just a subtle adjustment you didn't need experience to notice. I'd seen that kind of respect only a handful of times: not commanded, not demanded—earned.

One of the field training officers shouted, "Attention!"

Backs straight, heels locked—rookies snapping into place, doing their best to hide the nerves beneath the uniform. The line tightened because that's what you did when the people who would soon judge your every move stepped into view.

Even in that lineup, Top stood out, but not for anything loud or obvious.

The others brought structure; he brought something steadier—quiet, measured, and hard to ignore.

When he moved, attention followed him without a word being spoken.

"Parade rest," another FTO called, the command breaking the tension like a held breath finally released.

The movement was small, but it felt like permission to breathe again.

There was a steadiness in Top that made the rest of us measure ourselves. He came across like a drill sergeant who no longer needed volume to command a room. The squared shoulders, the controlled breathing, the composure shaped by years of repetition—discipline tempered, not displayed. As he shifted his arm, I caught a glimpse of ink disappearing beneath his sleeve—the kind of tattoo you don't choose; you earn.

Then the line inspection began.

The field training officers moved together, each stopping at a different rookie. Top took the far side, walking slow and deliberate, his eyes scanning uniforms the way a mechanic checks critical parts before an engine test.

A shoe that wasn't fully shined.

A smudge on a name tag.

A loose thread on a cuff.

He didn't raise his voice. He didn't need to.

"If you miss the small things on your uniform," he said quietly, stopping just long enough for the words to land, "you'll miss the small things that may save your life on the street."

Nobody shifted. Nobody swallowed. His attention made you stand straighter without knowing why.

And even though none of us said it out loud, we all registered the same truth as we stood shoulder to shoulder: Top understood the job in a way none of us could yet name.

A few days later, the street would prove him right.

* * *

Top's warning on that back lot stayed with me long after the cicadas quieted and the sunset fell on the town. It wasn't fear that settled in my chest that night—it was awareness. The academy taught procedure. I would learn later that Top taught perspective—the kind forged in places where procedure sometimes failed.

I didn't know yet what his calm had cost him. I didn't know what he had seen—or what he expected us to learn. I only knew that when he looked at you, he wasn't checking your polish or confidence. He was checking whether you would listen. Only much later would I understand the gravity behind that silence.

What We Saw

I rode with Top soon after graduation. His cruiser smelled of gun oil and strong coffee—the mix that became the scent of night work. My nerves made the air feel tighter than it should've been. The windows were cracked just enough for the air to slip in from the sound. His gear was laid out with ritual precision: flashlight parallel to the console, notebook open to a clean page, and radio clipped just so. A Bible rested in the cruiser's door pocket, the leather worn at the spine from quiet use.

"You don't get points for speed," he said, watching me fumble with the mic. "You get points for being calm."

His breathing never changed—slow, controlled, a metronome set against my pulse.

He let out a short laugh. "Everyone's useless the first week. The badge buys attention, not respect. You'll earn that one call at a time."

Ten minutes later, Dispatch sent us to a domestic disturbance. The adrenaline surge hit—heartbeat quick and loud. Top turned the wheel and said, "Slow down. Breathe. Think first."

As we stepped toward the doorway, he repeated it—quieter, steadier:

"Steady your feet before you step into someone else's storm."

I didn't know it then, but that line would come back to me more times than I could count.

A low fog spilled in from the sound, halos blooming around each porch light as we approached. The air pressed against my skin, carrying the faint scent of fried food and spilled beer—the kind of lived-in smell that told you trouble had been simmering long before the call.

A woman cried on the porch, shoulders shaking. Inside, a man's voice cracked furniture and distance. Glass shattered somewhere deeper in the house. Instinct pushed me forward.

Top raised a hand.

"Wait," he whispered. "If you rush into noise, you become part of it."

So we listened. A slammed cabinet. Heavy pacing. The kind of cursing that carried years behind it. Slowly the sound shifted—from sharp rage to ragged exhaustion. Only then did Top knock once, slow and measured.

"Never stand in front of the door, stand to the side. If they've got bad intentions, they might shoot through the door," he said. "You don't ever want to be standing in the blast."

Inside, his voice didn't rise; it settled. He stepped in steady, shoulders loose, eyes level. His stillness felt like authority without threat. He asked short questions and let silence do most of the work. Words replaced yelling until the room finally breathed again. No one went to jail, and no one got hurt.

"Not every win looks like an arrest," he said later. "Sometimes it looks like everyone staying alive."

We'd drilled the same breath control in defensive tactics and on the range—our instructors called it the only skill you can use on every call. With Top, it stopped being a training phrase and became muscle memory with purpose.

Something in me shifted that night—the rough edge inside me easing just enough to notice more and listen more.

The next morning, when I walked into the station, my reflection on the glass door looked different. Not proud. Not scared. Just more aware. I realized caution wasn't weakness—it was preparation.

*　*　*

Over the next few weeks, I learned that Top carried more than a gun and a radio. He carried experiences he rarely spoke about. He never bragged, but sometimes, when the radio went still, his eyes drifted somewhere far off. He'd start a story and stop halfway, jaw tightening for just a second—like something unwelcome had surfaced. The pause that followed felt heavier than the words he didn't say. Sometimes he cleared his throat—a small reset, as if pushing the memory back where it belonged.

Once I asked why he stayed on the job so long.

He stared through the windshield, streetlights sliding across his face. "Because someone has to teach you what the academy can't."

He tapped the steering wheel once. "You think you've seen desperation? Wait until you see what people do when they believe they've got nothing left. Sometimes they'll give everything. Sometimes they'll take everything." His tone wasn't dramatic—just factual.

That night, for the first time, I wrote his words in the small notebook I kept in my breast pocket, unsure if it was for study or survival. I didn't know then that I would fill dozens more before the career was done.

I still didn't know what courage was—only that it began after doubt, when you chose awareness over impulse.

One night, after a call that almost went bad but didn't, he looked at me and said, "You'll be fine. You think before you move. That's what keeps you human."

It sounded simple. It wasn't.

His lessons were quiet ones, and they worked slowly—changing me one shift at a time.

The Noise Inside You

Two weeks into field training, I was finally behind the wheel instead of riding shotgun when the radio erupted: "Shots fired. Road-rage incident. Vehicles stopped, Highway 70 near mile marker thirty-two."

Top's eyes met mine once, steady and unreadable. "Let's go," he said, as if we were heading to a noise complaint instead of a call threaded with gunfire.

The streets blurred in streaks of blue. Storefronts and pines flashed by in alternating shadows. As we left the slower roads near the waterfront, the highway opened ahead. My heart pounded so hard it felt like it wanted out of my chest. My hands tightened on the wheel before my brain could catch up, an instinct older than training. The world narrowed—dash lights, radio chatter, road—until his voice broke through, even and patient.

"The call will still be there when we arrive."

It wasn't a reprimand. It was an anchor. I eased off the accelerator. The engine dropped from a roar to a controlled growl. Headlights cut through the dark, catching white fence posts along the shoulder and the glint of shallow water in a ditch. One breath in, one out. Again. His calm settled across the cabin, smoothing the air between us.

Top never rushed. Urgency without panic—that was his gift. He made movement look like patience.

At the scene, two cars sat nose-to-nose, steam rising off bent hoods. Glass glittered across the highway like spilled ice. Gunpowder clung to the air, a bitter edge riding over the smell of exhaust. A man shouted behind one car, hands hidden. Another voice screamed nearby—high, panicked, unbroken.

Top stepped out first, moving like time itself had slowed to match him, firearm raised.

"Show me your hands," he said—firm, even, unshakable.

The man's eyes flicked to the gun lying near his feet. For a heartbeat, the world shrank to that stretch of ground between his fingers and the weapon. My own weapon was raised, steady but tight. I could hear my pulse louder than the approaching sirens. For a split second, I almost stepped in closer, closing the gap. Top's hand brushed my arm—barely a touch, but enough.

Only then did I realize I'd been about to put myself within reach of both the man and the gun.

"Hands," Top repeated, same tone, a decibel higher.

The man obeyed. Fingers up. Palms out. Top's composure pulled the chaos toward stillness. One command at a time, the scene unraveled back into something we could hold. We separated the drivers, checked for injuries, and secured the weapon.

No one was hurt. No one bled. No headlines. Just a moment that could have gone wrong in a dozen different ways and didn't.

Back at the cruiser, he looked at me. "You felt it, didn't you?"

I nodded.

"You almost rushed him," he said quietly. "Give a man too little room and he'll do something stupid just to feel free. Space is a tool—keep it until you're sure you don't need it."

He looked over, eyes steady.

"The adrenaline inside you is what you've really got to learn to fight."

For a long time after that night, I thought of it as something alive in my chest—a restless force testing the leash every time it rose inside of me. It was the feelings of urgency, instinct, ego, and uncertainty—all clamoring at once. Top never tried to kill it. He was teaching me how to make it listen.

He tapped his chest. "You can't control the world out there—only what happens in here. Master that, and you'll last."

Later, at a gas station over burnt coffee, he added, "Every officer gets scared, so don't believe the ones who show false bravado. The good ones just don't stay in that moment."

He wasn't wrong. The feelings don't vanish; they wait. That night I realized the feelings I was experiencing were less an enemy than an echo—proof that you were still paying attention.

On the drive back to the station, the hum of the cruiser steadied what was left of my pulse. I leaned into the rhythm, his words falling in step with the engine's low drone. Outside, wind slid across the water. Top watched the shoulder pass by, quiet as the turning tide—shoulders relaxed, one hand easy on the window frame. Whatever courage was, it lived somewhere between heartbeat and breath.

That week, I wrote in my notebook every night—short lines about what I'd seen, what I'd missed, what I'd felt, and what I hadn't yet understood. Top saw it once and smiled.

"Good. Write it down. The mind forgets what it's supposed to remember. Writing keeps the pressure from building."

That became habit—his kind of armor, even if I didn't fully understand it yet.

One night I reread my notes and saw a pattern. Every entry began with what I had done and ended with what Top had not. He didn't rush. He didn't raise his voice. He didn't lose the thread. The more I wrote, the more I realized the real lesson wasn't tactics. It was restraint.

By then, that hard pulse inside me didn't settle; it just stopped making decisions for me. Some nights it pressed against the edges of my focus, testing the seams. On better ones, it quieted and listened. And I understood—maybe for the first time—that control wasn't something you achieved. It was something you practiced, breath by breath, until the noise inside you learned who was in charge.

I'd walked into that shift thinking the job thrived on adrenaline—the chase, the flash, the danger. But riding with Top, the noise inside me settling into something slower, I finally understood that the job lived in the pauses—in the spacing between decisions, in the discipline you carried when no one was watching.

The next lessons wouldn't come from chaos at all.

They would come in the quiet work—the part of the job that shaped you long before the street ever tried.

The Work Beneath the Badge

Weeks blurred into one another, marked less by the calls themselves than by what Top taught in the spaces between them. After the call on Highway 70, the world felt different—less like a series of emergencies and more like a long stretch of subtle tests I didn't yet know how to measure. Top never said it outright, but every shift felt like he was showing me the job beneath the job, the version you couldn't learn from academy drills or laminated policy.

"Someone's always watching," he said once. "Even when they're not."

He had no patience for politics and even less for posturing. If you asked what he thought, you got it unvarnished. That honesty made him a headache to brass and a compass to the rest of us. He believed professionalism wasn't a performance for other people—it was a discipline you kept for yourself. Outer order protecting inner steadiness. I didn't fully understand it then, but I saw it in the way he checked his gear and the way he waited for a scene to breathe before he stepped into it.

If Top joked with you, it meant he trusted you enough to test your balance. The first time he did, I knew I'd passed some unspoken exam.

By week four, the shifts stitched themselves together, each one carrying its share of anger, fear, and grief.

Over the weeks, I learned to read the angle of Top's shoulders like a sentence. If he leaned forward, things were shifting. If he turned sideways to gain his center and casually unsnapped his handcuff case, someone had crossed a line. He didn't have to speak—the room adjusted before he did.

*   *   *

Sometimes the job didn't teach in moments—it taught in fragments. Small calls, small lessons, stitched together in the hours between midnight and dawn.

Child Welfare Check, 20:03.

A call from Social Services—welfare check on a child, reports of "unsanitary conditions." The porch light flickered over a yard scattered with weather-bleached toys. Inside, clutter pressed close, the air heavy with damp carpet and a stale sweetness.

Top stepped in like he was entering a library.

"Evening," he said, voice low.

A small boy peeked from behind a hallway wall, clutching a fire truck missing a wheel. Top crouched—not reaching, just meeting the kid's eyes.

"Good truck," he said. The boy nodded once, still watching him.

The social worker talked with the mother—exhausted, overwhelmed, trying. No violence. No drugs. No immediate danger. Just a family worn thin.

Disturbance, Corner Store, 22:10.

A man yelling, knocking items off a counter. Neon beer signs buzzed in the window, bleeding color across the linoleum. Top walked in like he was checking the weather.

"Store's closed," he said, even as the man puffed up and squared off.

Then—like steam venting from a valve—the man sagged. Top hadn't moved an inch. Stillness settled the room.

Back in the cruiser, he said, "Most folks carry things we can't see. If they're not drunk or dangerous, stand taller than their anger. They'll follow the shade."

Traffic Stop, 00:47.

A drifting car, fog hanging low in the headlamps. I expected a drunk; instead, a terrified college kid gripped the wheel while a wild-eyed cat hissed on the dash like it paid rent there. Top peered in and smirked.

"That cat looks meaner than half the people we haul in."

No ticket. Just a warning and a kid who stopped shaking.

"Most people you stop aren't criminals," he said as we drove off. "They're just trying to get through their night. Learn the difference."

Domestic, 02:19.

The kitchen was chaos—shattered plates and a child's cry from somewhere deeper in the house. My pulse begged me to rush in loud; Top put a hand on my arm.

"Breathe. Listen."

He set his hat on the counter, voice low.

"Mike, tell me what happened."

Names, stories, small talk about the kid's school—ordinary words in an extraordinary moment. Rage dissolved into exhaustion. No cuffs. Just a phone number on the counter and a promise to try again in the morning.

Outside, Top tapped his temple and his mouth.

"Your best tools," he said. "Head and voice. Use those first."

*　*　*

Later that week, we answered a welfare check—a veteran who hadn't been seen for days. The porch light buzzed but didn't warm anything. Inside, the house smelled of loneliness. The man sat in a recliner that sagged under the weight of years, his gaze fixed somewhere beyond us. Top spoke softly, calling him by name, and when the man finally opened the door, tears carved tracks down the dust on his face.

Top let out a quiet sigh—one he caught halfway, as if even that small slip needed permission. He stepped forward gently—not as an officer, but as someone who understood what it meant to carry battles no one else could see.

No report ever captured that part. The paper said no action was taken. But we both knew better.

After that, I stopped seeing calls as tests of authority and started seeing them as tests of patience and kindness. Top was teaching me how to make space where chaos wanted to close in—how to keep my voice steady when someone else's life shook apart. I realized the real work wasn't about what you did during the noise. It was how you carried yourself in the moments around it.

By then, the restless hum inside me no longer ran the room. Some nights it prowled. On better ones, it listened. Restraint was something you practiced until instinct learned its place.

That was when I noticed something else—not about me, but about him.

The way his eyes drifted after hard calls.

The stillness that lingered around him.

The stories he carried and never told.

That quiet strength wasn't free. It had been earned the long way.

Soon enough, I'd understand what it had cost him.

The Conversation in the Quiet Hours

The town folded into one of those pauses that felt rehearsed, as if the streets were holding their breath, waiting for a cue. Sidewalks empty. Storefronts dark. Porch lights glowing like small, stubborn lanterns against a world that was mostly asleep. Somewhere beyond the neighborhoods, the Atlantic breathed against the shore—a slow hush beneath everything, steady as a pulse. The kind of quiet that made you check the rearview mirror twice, not for danger, but just to be sure the world was still moving around you.

Top cracked the window and thumbed a Marlboro from the pack. When he flicked the lighter, the flame danced in the reflection of the windshield—small, bright, alive—casting a brief glow across his face before settling into a slow burn at the tip of the cigarette. Smoke curled into the damp air with a faint metallic hint that always seemed to linger after long shifts. He exhaled once, slow, and gave me that sidelong glance—half warning, half invitation—the one that said, "This part never makes it into the manuals."

"This job," he said, voice gravel-thick from smoke and years, "will bore you to death before it ever tries to kill you. Hours of nothing. Empty streets. People asleep while we drive circles through the dark."

He snapped his fingers—sharp, sudden, and clean as a gunshot. "And then, pure terror. No warning. One heartbeat you're half-asleep, the next your chest feels like it's going to split open. That's the rhythm. Boredom. Terror. Back and forth."

I nodded, though nodding felt too small for the gravity of what he was saying. My chest tightened anyway, because I could feel the truth of it settling into me—the shots fired call on Highway 70, the domestic calls, the quiet check-ins that turned when you least expected. Every shift felt like a coin flip with no warning which side would land face-up.

"The trick," he went on, smoke drifting past the dash in a thin silver ribbon, "is living in both. Don't get sloppy in the quiet. Don't freeze in the storm. Pull that off, and you'll last. Fail, and this job will chew you up."

He looked back toward the empty street, eyes following the faint flicker of a dying streetlamp. "You'll know you're getting better when the lull feels like work… and chaos feels like routine."

The cruiser hummed on, tires droning against the asphalt like a heartbeat in the dark. Every mailbox we passed felt like a chapter in someone else's story. Houses drifted past in slow motion—kitchens lit by the glow of a refrigerator, silhouettes moving behind blinds, and porch flags shifting in the breeze. Lives we'd never enter unless something had already gone wrong.

I realized then that he wasn't offering advice—not really. He was handing me a warning wrapped in smoke and silence, something earned the hard way. Something he knew I'd have to carry sooner or later.

When he finished his cigarette, he tapped the ash against the window frame, its embers scattering briefly before the wind swallowed them.

"Most people never understand what we really do," he said softly. "That's all right. It's not their burden to carry."

He rolled the window up, sealing the quiet back inside the cruiser. The world resumed its slow turn—the kind you could feel more than hear.

And in that small, flickering moment between his words and the hum of the engine, I understood something I hadn't before: chaos might test you, but the quiet hours built whatever would meet that chaos.

And Top… he carried more than calm into those hours.

Much more.

What Top Carried

Everyone liked Top, even the ones who pretended not to. Dispatchers trusted his voice. New officers leaned in when he spoke. Old-timers nodded when he walked into a room. In a fight, in an alley, in that half-second when instinct collides with training, Top was the man you wanted at your shoulder. He never demanded respect—he radiated it, steady as heat rising from asphalt after a long day.

Sometimes, when the radio went quiet, I'd catch him rolling his shoulder where the Marine Corps flag lived under his sleeve. Not a wince—just memory checking in. That small motion told more than words ever could. He carried things he would never name, the kind that settled into your posture one block at a time. Some burdens you carry. Others settle so deep they change the way you stand. Watching him, I began to understand that his control wasn't performed; it was forged in places harder than these streets. And without realizing it, I was learning how to carry it.

He kept a single photograph tucked into the visor, a black-and-white of four Marines in front of a sandbag wall. Their smiles were thin, their uniforms dusted thick enough to blur the color beneath. When the light caught it once, I asked if it was him.

He said, "Was," and closed the visor. That was the end of the conversation. The way he shut it told me the picture wasn't nostalgia—it was a ledger entry. A reminder of who didn't make it home. A reminder of why he refused to get sloppy, even on the quiet nights.

By week six, I understood what the academy could never teach. A badge is issued, but it's only earned when the street trusts you. And the street doesn't trust easily. It watches the way you walk into a scene, the way you handle a raised voice, and the way you breathe when the world begins to tilt. I didn't know it then, but every time Top watched me take a call, he wasn't judging my decisions—he was deciding whether the town would eventually accept me as one of its own.

The academy had given me a uniform. Top taught me how to wear it. How to keep my hands steady when someone else's world was breaking apart. How to listen when noise begged me to act. How to move when fear rooted others in place. Like the scar he carried, the lessons he left in me were permanent. They rooted deep, stitching themselves beneath the surface until instinct and guidance became the same thing.

Top didn't talk about control. He lived it—quietly, consistently, like breath. And because I stood beside him long enough, that steadiness bled into me without ceremony, the way light drifts across a wall. Control wasn't a skill. It was something passed hand-to-hand through moments you barely noticed until they shaped you.

The first time he said nothing after a call, I knew I'd done something right. Silence was his version of trust. That silence stayed with me longer than any praise ever could. It felt like a weight settling on my shoulders—but not the crushing kind. More like the responsibility of choosing a place to rest.

Soon enough, the silence would be mine to fill. I'd drive alone—Top's lessons echoing where fear used to sit, his steadiness working its way into my breath, my thoughts, and my grip on the wheel.

Alone in the dark is where you learn which parts of your training were academic—and which parts someone gave you because they knew you'd need them to survive.

Top taught me how to quiet the noise inside me, but he couldn't walk the next miles for me. Every officer meets that moment alone, and mine was already on its way.

And soon, the night would ask me to prove it.

Chapter 3—Alone in the Dark

We suffer more often in imagination than in reality.

—Seneca

Some endings don't announce themselves; they arrive gradually, in the pauses between calls, taking shape while you're busy looking the other way. After weeks with Top riding shotgun, I could feel something shifting, even if no one said it out loud. The nights grew more controlled, almost intentional, as if he were stepping back an inch at a time and watching whether I could fill the space he left. His silence was changing shape. It no longer guided; it evaluated.

By then I'd learned that his real lessons didn't come from the chaos— they came from the stillness, in those quiet minutes after a call when you're left alone with your thoughts, your pulse, and the ghosts that trail behind you.

Every officer reaches a night when borrowed calm won't carry you anymore—when the town asks whether you can stand on your own feet. By that point, even the air felt heavier—electric, watchful, holding its own kind of breath. I didn't know it yet, but I was heading straight toward that moment. Before the sun came up again, I'd face the parts of the job the academy never warned us about—the darkness in the houses we stepped into and the quiet unrest that waited inside me.

Final Ride with Top

Something about the night felt different before anything happened.

We were parked at our usual late-night diner, the kind that smelled like bacon grease, burnt toast, and whatever the grill had given up on hours earlier. The cook waved through the window, the kind of man who'd seen enough cops to know when to keep the griddle hot and the questions few. Top stirred his coffee slowly, eyes on the street instead of on me. The silence around him felt heavier, more intentional than usual.

"You think you're ready to be by yourself?"

I shrugged, feeling the familiar knot in my stomach. "Doesn't feel real."

He didn't reply right away. He just watched the traffic light cycle from red to green and back again, the glow washing across his face. "It never does," he said finally. Then he dropped a couple of dollars on the table and stood. "Let's see what the night thinks."

Outside, the air carried the smell of rain on metal. The cruiser door creaked as it shut, and the radio whispered with the static of other people's trouble. My palms were warm against the cold steering wheel. A quiet tension settled in the cab, the kind of stillness waiting for something to tilt.

"Unit 819, respond. Subject: trespassing. Refusing to leave."

The address made my chest tighten. One of the roughest areas in town—the kind of place you never went in alone.

A row of motorcycles leaned like sentries out front, chrome catching the porch light. The apartment sat dark, arranged in a way that felt wrong—you could feel eyes watching before you found them.

Top glanced over, calm as ever. "You take the lead," he said. "I'm just here for backup."

He made it sound routine, but it wasn't. It was a test.

A porch light flickered. A curtain twitched. A man in his early thirties stepped out barefoot and shirtless.

"Man, I don't want you to arrest her," he said. "I just need her gone. She's drunk. I gotta work in the morning."

I peered past him into the shadows. The air drifting out was thick with sour liquor, stale smoke, and something sharp and metallic underneath it.

"Where is she now?"

He jerked a thumb toward the back. "When she saw y'all pull up, she ran out the back door."

"So she's not here?"

"No, sir."

"Then lock your doors. Don't let her back in."

We cleared the call and rolled out. My pulse stayed high—higher than the facts justified. Top didn't comment. He didn't need to. The night was still catching up with my nerves.

Five minutes later, dispatch snapped back through the static—same address.

This time, the man stumbled out with blood running from his nose and lip. "Dude, I don't want her here. Just make her leave."

Again, he swore she'd bolted when we arrived.

We cleared the scene a second time and pulled away, gravel crunching under the tires as the apartment shrank in the mirror. Something about the man's earlier nerves stayed with me—a tightness in his voice I still couldn't name.

Before I could shift into drive, the radio flared again:

"Unit 819, return to that apartment. Third call. Subject still refusing to leave."

The man met us at the door, his face bloody and his shoulders sagging like he'd aged ten years in half an hour.

"She's in the apartment. Back bedroom. I don't want you to arrest her. I just want her out."

Inside, the apartment reeked of grease, sweat, and stale liquor. A half-disassembled motorcycle sprawled across the kitchen table, bolts scattered like dice after a bad roll.

"Which room?"

He pointed down the hallway. "Back there. She doesn't have clothes on."

The air felt thick as I approached the door. I braced and flicked the switch. The bulb flared, exposing a woman in her late twenties. She shot upright, dragging the blanket to her chest.

"What the fuck are you doing in here? Get the fuck out!"

"Ma'am," I said evenly, "he doesn't want you here. You need to get dressed and leave." I told her again. Then again.

The standoff stretched—a taut wire between us. Her words were sharp; mine were flat. Then she erupted from the bed with frightening speed, her hands wrapping around my throat. Her fingers dug in, her nails scraping just enough to sting, choking off breath.

Instinct took over. I grabbed the back of her neck and drove her to the floor. She screamed. The carpet tore at my knees, the blanket twisting between us like useless armor. My focus tightened, the world narrowing to nothing but grip, balance, and breath.

Top never moved. He leaned in the doorway, arms folded, his eyes steady.

"You gonna let her get dressed first?" he asked, voice dry as dust.

"Nope," I said, tightening the cuffs. "Gave her plenty of chances."

He didn't argue. I walked her out—naked, furious, cuffed—the night cold enough to raise goosebumps on both of us.

By the time we reached the car, my pulse had slowed into that shaky calm.

Top pulled the cruiser's back door open without a word.

We cleared the scene in silence. Top's gaze stayed fixed on the road ahead. His calm steadied the cab the way ballast steadies a ship. When he finally spoke, it was barely above the hum of the tires.

"Next time," he said quietly, "anticipate what they're about to do. You did good—but talk them down if you can. Sometimes that buys you all the space you need. Words are cheaper than stitches."

I nodded. The lesson sank in deeper than the bruises forming on my neck. Every measured mile beside him was rehearsal for the silence that would follow. One day, that calm would be mine to carry—and my rookies would hear it the same way I once did. But before I could pass anything on, I had to feel what that silence was like with no one in the seat beside me.

*   *   *

By the time we reached the Magistrate's office, it was wall-to-wall chaos. Officers shoulder-to-shoulder with arrestees, paperwork flying, voices ricocheting off tile and cinderblock. Sweat, coffee, and cheap disinfectant hung in the air. I sat her on the bench, and the room froze. Heads turned. Whispers cut the noise down to a hum.

The Magistrate's eyes widened. "Officer… why is that woman naked?"

I kept my voice steady. "She refused to get dressed. Then she assaulted me."

The magistrate blinked once and sighed. "Fine. She can sit there until she's called."

And that's how she sat: cuffed, exposed, waiting in the middle of intake until a jailer brought in a sheet.

The veteran sergeant sitting beside me raised an eyebrow. "First naked arrest?" he said under his breath.

"Hopefully the last," I said, though even then I wasn't sure.

He grinned. "Don't bet on it."

Later, after clearing the jail, I found Top leaning against the hood of the car, the parking lot light carving his face into shadow. He gave me one slow nod. No words. Just approval.

That nod meant more than any commendation. It was a quiet transfer of trust—the leash coming off.

He looked at me once more before climbing into his car. "You did fine," he said. "Now don't screw it up."

In that moment, I didn't need him to say I was ready.

I believed it.

Driving back to the station, I realized the night hadn't tested whether I could handle danger—it had tested whether I could handle myself.

Badge, Keys, Go

The next shift should've been routine with Top. We'd just come off a few days' rest and were easing back into the rhythm of nights when the Chief called me at home. Even before I picked up, my stomach tightened—the last thing you ever want is a call from the Chief. Seeing his name on the caller ID only made it worse. He told me to come in early—then said nothing else. Just silence. No explanation, no hint, no tone to read.

The house felt hollow after the line went dead, the kind of quiet that stretched long enough to make you hear your own heartbeat. As I grabbed my gear, I caught myself pausing at the door, hearing Top's voice in the back of my mind: Slow the hands. Clear the mind. It didn't stop the worry, but it steadied the next breath.

Driving to the station, I imagined worst-case endings—turning in my badge before I'd cleared probation, some mistake I didn't know I'd made. Every red light felt like judgment; every reflection in the windshield looked like a version of myself I wasn't ready to meet. By the time I turned onto the street that led to the station, the silence riding beside me felt almost human—shaped by dread and by the strange awareness that something was ending, whether I was ready for it or not.

When I walked through the station doors, the truth landed hard. Top had recommended I be released from training. He said I was ready. The Chief didn't waste time with speeches. He reached into his pocket, pulled out a set of keys, and tossed them through the air.

They hit my palm with a cold, decisive weight—a burden disguised as metal.

I didn't realize until that moment how heavy responsibility could feel when it fit inside a key ring.

"Your patrol car," he said. "Go out and enforce the law."

The words struck deeper than I expected. For the first time, I wasn't riding shotgun or waiting for cues. The streets were mine now. Every call, every decision, every mistake—they all had my name on them. Every rookie waits for this moment. None of us truly understand it until it arrives.

Later I'd learn the Chief retired from the Marines as a Gunnery Sergeant—a Gunny to his core—and he brought every inch of that into the Chief's office. Gunny Sergeants don't lose their habits; they just change the scenery. He took real pride in torturing his people long before he ever put on a police uniform, and he hadn't slowed down since. He mastered the art of deliberate silence—leaning back in his chair, letting the moment stretch just long enough to make you wonder what you'd missed. Half of it was discipline. The other half was pure Marine humor sharpened by decades of watching recruits sweat.

* * *

I'd spent eight weeks beside Top, learning the town the way you learn a scar on your own skin—the problem houses, the corners that never slept, the people who dialed 911 like ordering takeout. Eight weeks of patrol routes, report writing, and absorbing the rhythm of nights. And just as important, eight weeks of watching the people who wore the same patch, each of them carrying their own version of the job.

Some nights I caught myself glancing at the empty seat even before it was empty, wondering what it would feel like to drive alone. I could still hear Top's voice—steady, patient, hovering at the edge of thought like a metronome half a heartbeat behind my pulse.

The manuals said one thing.

The street said another.

Top always trusted the street.

He taught with silence—lessons tucked between the nods, the raised eyebrow, and the stillness he carried like a second uniform. If he said nothing at all, it meant you'd finally gotten it right. I could still hear him in my head: Slow the hands. Clear the mind. Let the scene come into focus.

* * *

We weren't a platoon marching in step. "Squad" didn't quite fit either. We were a rotation—names shuffled by a schedule that felt more like a test of endurance than anything tactical. Three on, two off. Four on, three off. Seven on, seven off. On paper it looked balanced. To the body, it was punishment.

By the time you adjusted to seven straight, the seven-off vanished like a thief in the morning light. You'd just start feeling human again, and suddenly you were back in the uniform. Brutal on the body. Worse on marriages. I watched more than one officer's home life fray or they would turn to a vice under the weight of a calendar that never matched anyone else's.

But the schedule had perks. Line it right, and a week of vacation stretched into nearly three. Long enough to breathe air that didn't smell like adrenaline. Long enough to pretend you lived a normal life.

Our town slept in uneven breaths—industrial on one side, ocean-flat on the other, smelling of salt, diesel, and the shad factory when the wind was wrong. When that plant ran hot, you avoided that side of town; the fish stench clung to your clothes like a curse. At night, the smokestacks stained the clouds a rusted red, and the hum of the highway threaded through every block. You judged the town's mood as much by sound as by sight.

Most nights, though, weren't scenic. There were fluorescent squad-room lights buzzing overhead, burnt coffee coating your tongue, and the fight to stay awake at 03:00 when the world outside your cruiser belonged to someone else.

Then came the night when the seat beside me stopped belonging to Top.

It was empty now—empty in a way that made the whole cruiser feel larger, like the air itself had shifted roles. And somewhere in that space, a different kind of quiet settled—one I'd have to learn to carry alone.

The streets didn't change that night. But the weight of them did.

Some shifts test your judgment. Some test your calm. Some test your resolve.

My first night alone would test something deeper—how you face the parts of the job no one warns you about until you're the one standing in the doorway.

The Seat Beside Me

The first night I rode alone felt like crossing a finish line I'd been running toward for weeks.

I'd earned the seat, the keys, and the responsibility that came with both. For the first time, every call, every outcome, every consequence belonged to me—and I wanted it that way. The hum of the cruiser sounded different when it was my cruiser.

I rolled out of the parking lot with a steadier pulse than I expected, a mix of nerves and pride and the thrill of finally being trusted to carry the night myself.

A few blocks in, though, I noticed the empty seat. The space where someone used to steady my hands or offer a quick correction was now just vinyl and silence. The cruiser felt bigger than before: not heavier, just mine.

The habits drilled over weeks showed up on their own: calm, patience, and breath before the move. I didn't need anyone beside me to call them out anymore.

Outside the cruiser, the road stretched into a darkness that didn't care who you were. The headlights reached the edge of the pines, then disappeared—leaving only the drone of tires and the soft rattle of gear in the trunk.

The first call came fast. A welfare check—simple on paper.

A neighbor hadn't seen the man next door in days. The dispatcher's tone was flat but careful.

I pulled up to a sagging ranch house with drawn blinds and a broken porch light. Frost glinted on the railings. That's when I realized I'd forgotten my flashlight. Rookie mistake. My stomach dropped as I keyed the mic for a check-in officer.

When she arrived, I felt a small, unspoken relief. She wasn't a rookie, just a year or so ahead. Together we circled the house, our boots crunching on frozen grass.

The back door hung crooked, unlocked. When I pushed it open, it groaned like it was alive.

We paused on the threshold, listening. The house smelled faintly of wax candles. Furniture sat where it had always sat. A calendar hung on the wall, pages still turned to the current week. A clock clicked loudly from the kitchen. Nothing looked abandoned. Nothing looked wrong.

We called out anyway. Loud. Clear. Again.

No response.

My pulse ticked up—not panic, just alertness. We moved room to room, voices high, our movements deliberate. A television flickered silently in the living room, closed captions crawling across the screen. A recliner faced it, worn smooth at the arms.

That's when the man stirred.

He rose slowly from the chair, startled, eyes wide, hands lifting in reflex more than fear. For a half-second, everything froze—the kind of moment training exists for. I eased my hands open, lowered my voice, and let the tension drain instead of rise.

He hadn't heard us. His hearing aids sat on the end table beside him, neatly placed, batteries out. He blinked, then smiled with a kind of relieved embarrassment.

"Didn't mean to scare you," I said.

We explained why we were there. The neighbor. The concern. The check. He nodded, understanding settling in as quickly as the surprise had faded. He thanked us more than once, the way people do when they realize someone noticed their absence.

We cleared the call. My voice was steadier now, the words routine even as the moment still felt fresh. It wasn't the kind of call you tell stories about. No sirens. No resolution that felt earned through action.

But as I pulled away, I understood something I hadn't before. Carrying the night wasn't just about what you ran toward. Sometimes it was about knocking, waiting, and being willing to scare someone just long enough to make sure they were still there.

Shadows at the Edge of the Light

The next night felt long but not dramatic. The wind off the water was cold and steady, cutting across the road and pushing mist low in thin, restless sheets. The inlet lay dark and flat beside us, black and reflective, giving nothing back. My cruiser moved through it slowly, headlights narrowing the world to pavement, marsh grass, and breath.

That's when the radio broke in.

"Unit 819, respond to a trespasser. Man seen in abandoned home."

Trespass calls were common enough to blur together, but they never felt routine. People without places drift toward whatever shelter they can find—under bridges, in empty boats, tucked into forgotten houses left standing long after the reason for them is gone. Those calls carried a quiet weight, the kind that settled in before you even stepped out of the cruiser.

We pulled up to a Victorian on the water, big once, impressive in another life. Now it sagged under its own age, porch slumping, windows dark, heat long gone. The air smelled of mildew and old fabric. Inside, furniture sat where it had been left, not arranged so much as abandoned— velvet chairs dulled by dust, curtains stiff at the edges, and picture frames clouded with fingerprints. Neighbors said the woman who lived there had died with no family to claim it, leaving the house behind to wait on nothing.

We entered through the back door, moving openly. The house wasn't active enough to hide anything. We cleared the first floor slowly. Nothing but our boots and the hollow sound of rooms answering back.

The stairs complained under our weight. Wood popped. My keys rattled against the banister, louder than I wanted. Not stealthy. Not meant to be.

Second floor—empty.

Then the third.

Something shifted ahead of us—a faint scrape across the floorboards, just enough to register. My pulse tightened. My backup eased the bedroom door open, and moonlight spilled across the rug through a broken window. Dust hung in the beam, drifting as we stepped inside.

It wasn't the house.

It was him.

He screamed—high and sharp—and the sound emptied him before he could stop it. It ricocheted off the walls and slammed into my chest, freezing me harder than anything in that room ever could have. For a split second, everything locked up—the kind of pause training exists for.

"What is it?" I managed, breath tight.

Embarrassed, he pointed—pale as the walls.

"That damn bird."

A skinny seagull sat on the dresser, feathers ruffled, head cocked like it had been personally offended by the attention.

Relief hit hard and messy. Our laughter came out rough—too loud, too sharp—bouncing off the ceiling and shaking dust loose. He never lived that scream down. I started calling him Fly-Guy after that, and the name followed him for years.

Standing there with cold air pushing through broken panes and the house settling under its own weight, I noticed my hands were still tight. Not fear—just the residue of it. The kind that lingers after your body reacts before your thoughts catch up.

By the time we stepped outside, the Victorian's silence clung to me again—subtle, persistent. The house looked unchanged. Dark. Empty. Still waiting. But the tension didn't stay behind with it. It rode with me when I pulled back onto the road, sitting low and unnoticed, like static you only hear once the volume drops.

The road opened up again, dark and empty. I settled back into the seat and kept going.

Three Shadows and a Wheelbarrow

Winter settled into the coast before I fully realized it. One week folded into the next, and the nights grew sharper—clean, cold edges that cut straight through the uniform. The tourists were long gone, boardwalk shutters pulled tight, and the town breathed in slow drafts that made the darker hours feel wider than they had a month earlier.

One of those nights, I was parked at the edge of town where the road bent into a long, sweeping curve. It was a good place to watch for drunk drivers—tucked away, quiet, the kind of spot where headlights announced themselves before the car did. The cruiser idled, a steady rumble that could lull you to sleep if you let it.

I lifted the binoculars and tracked the occasional car slipping through the bend, each set of headlights carving a clean arc across the pavement. The night felt routine, almost calm—just the cold, the curve, and the engine humming low.

Then something moved.

A shadow shifted beneath the parking deck.

Then another.

I lowered the binoculars and waited. Fatigue has a way of turning stillness into motion, of letting the mind fill in gaps that aren't really there. I raised them again. A third shape slid into view.

This wasn't that.

I eased the cruiser into drive, lights off, and crept toward the condos. I tucked in behind a row of hedges and killed the engine. The night rushed back in. I rolled down the window and listened. The wind carried surf rolling in—steady, distant—and beneath it, something else.

"Dispatch, send me a check-in."

Movement again.

I stepped out and eased up to the hedges, unholstering as I went. Three figures paused beneath the deck. One lifted a hand.

"Hold up. I hear something."

I stayed still. The sound came again—a faint, rhythmic squeak. Metal on metal.

A wheelbarrow.

They stepped out into the open, pushing it toward a waiting car. My stomach tightened. This wasn't kids sneaking into the pool. This was deliberate—planned and quick.

"Police! Let me see your hands! Get on the ground!"

They dropped immediately.

As I moved in, glass glittered across the pavement—car windows punched out clean, fragments scattered like ice. I keyed my shoulder mic. "10-18. Suspects at gunpoint." Backup was three minutes out, coming from the neighboring town.

Three minutes can stretch when you're alone.

I kept my voice even. Hands visible. Knees down. Stay right there. The night pressed in around us, quiet but alert. Somewhere far off, sirens rose and fell—too distant to count on, close enough to keep everyone listening.

The seconds passed one instruction at a time. No one bolted. No one tested the space. My breathing stayed slow and deliberate. The edge didn't go away, but it stopped pushing forward.

When the blue lights finally crested the road, the moment loosened. Not all at once—just enough. We cuffed the three beneath the deck, then the fourth waiting in the car. Broken glass, stolen property, wheelbarrow and all.

Standing there in the cold, blue lights washing concrete and faces flat, I noticed how quiet my hands were. The moment had come and gone, and I was still standing where I'd started.

The lessons had held.

So had I.

*   *   *

Later, back in the cruiser, the road felt narrower than before. Familiar, but sharpened. The curve where I'd been parked slipped past again, empty now, like nothing had ever happened.

By Saturday night, that awareness was still there—not loud, not urgent. Just present. The kind that sits with you. No warning. Just the moment you look up and realize you're already standing in it.

Saturday Night Shift

Saturday nights always carried a different voltage—an undercurrent you could feel before you ever keyed the mic. I'd barely stepped into the station when it hit me: that charged stillness that settles right before a shift decides what kind of night it will be. The moon outside was full and bright enough to wash the parking lot, the kind of light that made everything look sharper than it really was. You could almost believe the night would fly by.

I didn't even make it to the coffee pot.

One of the narcotics detectives stepped in—the kind of guy who didn't bother with greetings. He just jerked his chin toward the door.

"Need a hand serving a warrant," he said, as casually as asking someone to pass the bread.

The suspect was a familiar name—fresh out of prison and already drifting back into the same dark current that had dragged him under the first time. The only place we could predictably find him was at work: a hole-in-the-wall restaurant on the waterfront. The kind of place that smelled of fryer grease, bleach, and sweat baked into the walls. The back door stayed propped open with a brick, dumping steam into the night like the building itself was exhaling.

We went in through the kitchen.

He stood at the sink with sleeves rolled high, tattoos climbing his neck, and arms thick from years of lifting more than dishes.

"Evening," the detective said. "We've got a warrant for your arrest. I told you I'd be seeing you soon."

The man froze, water running over his hands like he didn't quite belong in his own skin. He turned slowly, eyes flat—not scared, just measuring. He'd done this before. He knew how quickly moments like this could collapse.

He muttered something I couldn't hear and backed toward a supply closet. That's when I saw his hand close around a can of drain cleaner. The label flashed under the fluorescent lights.

"If you get close," he said, voice low and steady, "I'm throwing this in your face."

He wasn't blustering. It was a decision forming.

The detective's gun cleared leather before the sentence finished.

"Put it down," he said—sharp but calm, a tone shaped by repetition more than emotion. "I will shoot you."

The man stopped. You could see him running the math—distance, angles, outcomes—understanding exactly where he stood.

The kitchen fan hummed. Water hissed against metal. Employees froze. The space narrowed to what mattered.

"Dispatch, send additional units—10-18."

The man set the cleaner down and stepped away.

But he wasn't finished.

He pivoted and lunged toward the back door, muscles coiling like he meant to force an exit—or test us trying. I moved in, reached for his arm—and my feet left the floor. The floor came up fast and unforgiving, throwing me hard, knocking the breath from my lungs.

Training took over before thought could.

I surged up, wrapped my arms around his chest, and held on as he bucked and twisted. Pots rattled. Plates crashed. The detective locked onto his other arm. Another officer rushed in, then another. The fight compressed into movement and leverage.

It took six of us and two sets of cuffs.

When it was over, the kitchen looked like we'd dragged weather through it—chairs overturned, water everywhere, steam hanging thick in the air. That bright white can of drain cleaner sat untouched on the shelf.

Outside, the world kept moving. Cars rolled down the highway. The moon still hung over the water, bright and indifferent. I stood in the parking lot catching my breath, aware—again—of how discipline, timing, and restraint decide outcomes long before paperwork ever does.

That's the part the academy rarely lingers on.

Some nights don't announce themselves with noise.

They test whether you're ready.

The lesson was familiar: the night doesn't reward hesitation, but it doesn't forgive recklessness either.

I drove for a while, letting the silence settle back into its proper place. With every mile, the call faded into the steady rhythm of tires over pavement. The town thinned as I approached the harbor—fewer lights, wider shadows, the air shifting to the smell of damp wood. Boats rocked in their slips, lines groaning softly, resisting the pull of the tide.

Nights like that don't end when the cuffs click.

They stay with you—quiet, measured—waiting to see what you carry forward into the next one.

The House That Watched the Harbor

The town looked larger and sharper that night. The glow from storefront windows felt distant, the stoplights too slow, and every alley seemed to breathe on its own. I turned down a narrow street near Taylor's Creek, where old Victorian houses stood shoulder to shoulder; their porches bowed from the years. The wind off the sound was sharp enough to cut, carrying the smell of marshland.

Most of the shops were closed for the season—cold, dark, wrapped in that lull a town settles into when it exhales and waits for spring.

Local legend says one of those houses once belonged to Blackbeard. Top had told me the story one night—his voice flat and serious, though the glint in his eye made me wonder if he was testing me. He said the pirate used to stand on the second-story porch, looking out over the creek, counting the masts of his ships as they swayed in the moonlight.

The story, like most old ones, had teeth. Some said he murdered a young woman in the parlor, her blood leaving stains that came and went with the tides. Others swore he had one of his wives hanged from a live oak in the yard, her spirit drifting through the branches when the wind blew right.

I slowed the cruiser and stared at the house. It didn't look cursed. It looked beautiful—white columns leaning slightly, shutters half-closed, a porch swing moving once, slow and aimless, though there was no breeze. The moonlight caught the second-story windows just enough to make it seem as if someone were standing there, watching the water.

A chill ran through me—not from the cold, but from the kind of unease older places know how to hold. The same feeling you get clearing a long hallway or standing a moment too long at a door cracked open and waiting.

I'd never seen a ghost, and I didn't plan to start that night. But I didn't shrug it off either. Some stories don't need telling. They just ask for distance.

I eased the car forward, headlights sweeping across the porch, catching the edges of white paint and weathered wood. The swing shifted again, slow and deliberate, as if saying goodbye.

As I drove away, I thought about how every officer carries a ghost story of their own—something you can't prove but still believe enough not to test. Maybe one day I'd pass that story on to a rookie, watch her expression in the mirror, and see if she flinched. Unease comes in many forms. Sometimes it looks like a pirate's house on a cold winter night. Sometimes it rides beside you, quiet and waiting for the call that makes it real.

The Longest Hours

The hours between 02:00 and 05:00 feel like a kind of purgatory. The bar fights are done. The early walkers aren't awake yet. What's left are the lonely, the lost, and the dying—people whose lives drift quietly at the margins while the rest of the world sleeps. Those hours stretch thin and smear together, testing whether you can stay alert when the town seems content to forget you exist. They teach patience, or they break you.

After the Blackbeard house, I didn't want to go back to the station. The idea of fluorescent lights and half-awake chatter felt wrong after standing in the shadow of something that old and silent. Instead, I pulled into a convenience-store lot and killed the engine. The windows fogged with my breath, softening the streetlight outside into a damp halo. The clerk inside was wiping down the counters.

I sat there, letting the radio murmur while the clipboard rested against my knee, the paper whispering as I wrote. My handwriting looked unsteady under the dome light—too sharp in some places, too hesitant in others.

Quiet is deceptive. The town's heartbeat never really stops; it just slows down to see who's paying attention. That night, I finally understood what Top meant when he said the street teaches its own lessons. Silence wasn't a release—it was pressure.

A trawler moaned beyond the docks, its low hum rolling through the fog like a memory refusing to sleep. Sirens drifted from somewhere deeper in the town—another medical call swallowed by the dark. Even the wind seemed to move differently, slower, as if it too were caught between worlds.

Loneliness doesn't arrive all at once. It seeps into the pauses between calls, into the moments when your headlights skim across empty porches and closed curtains. People wave when they need you and vanish when they don't. Even the other officers—the ones who understand—are scattered across the town in their own cruisers, connected only by radio clicks.

The radio came to life.

"Unit 819, respond. Noise complaint, domestic in progress."

My pulse jumped before my mind caught up. Another domestic. Somehow it felt fitting—my first night alone circling back to a familiar storm that had taught me to slow down.

The address was across town—different faces, same script.

I parked across the street, headlights off, the cruiser blacked out and angled so I could watch the house without becoming part of the scene. The front door stood wide open, yellow light spilling across the porch. Shouts overlapped inside—fast, sharp, and jagged. Only a thin screen door held the chaos inside.

A minute later, my backup pulled in behind me. Brand-new uniform. Brand-new confidence. His engine was still ticking when he jumped out.

He started toward the porch, shoulders high, eyes locked on the doorway—moving fast.

"Hang on," I said, catching his arm before he could charge straight into someone else's storm. "Breathe. Slow down. Never run into a domestic blind."

He swallowed hard and nodded once. His boots stopped trying to outrun his pulse.

Only then did we move together.

The porch boards creaked under our weight, and the shouting inside cut off like someone had pulled a plug. A woman stood near the couch, wiping her mouth with the back of her hand. A man hovered by the kitchen entry, staring at the floor—ashamed, angry, and exhausted, maybe all three.

I eased the screen door open.

"Police. Separate," I said evenly. "Now."

They listened. Habit. Fatigue. Or maybe the uniform still carried weight in those thin hours when the world tilts quiet.

I talked to each of them while the rookie hovered within arm's reach—watching, learning, slowing down. I wrote what needed writing and watched the adrenaline drain from their bodies until the room settled into something that resembled calm, at least from a distance.

No injuries. No assault. No jail.

Just another small disaster steadied with space, patience, and a steady voice.

Walking back to the cruiser, I realized I hadn't just remembered Top's lessons that night—I'd acted on them without thinking.

Clearing the call, the dispatcher's voice crackled through the back channel.

"Good work, 819."

Not praise. Just acknowledgment. Sometimes that was enough.

I told myself I was calm, but my hands hadn't caught up yet.

Down the block, beneath a flickering streetlight, insects hurled themselves at the bulb—drawn to a heat that would burn them if they got too close. It reminded me of us, moving toward chaos because we were trained to, even knowing exactly how hot it could get.

The vinyl seat creaked beneath me.

The night pressed in around the cruiser—dim, breathless, watchful.

And just when the quiet felt like it might swallow the rest of the shift whole, the radio cracked open again.

Not loud.

Not urgent.

Just enough to let me know the dark wasn't finished yet.

The next call was coming.

And it carried a different kind of weight.

The Stop at 03:00

The late shift has its own kind of silence.

By three in the morning, most of the town was asleep. The bars had emptied, the traffic lights cycled through their colors for no one, and the highway hummed with the occasional semi sliding through on its way to somewhere else. The air that night was still and thick—late-spring Carolina—warm enough for the cruiser's A/C to rattle in protest, cool enough for fog to curl low over the ditches.

I cruised a stretch of four-lane that almost never gave me trouble. Windows up, radio low, headlights cutting a clean tunnel of pale yellow through the dark. Not peace—just the quiet that settles after days spent running toward other people's storms.

Then headlights crested the hill ahead—too fast.

A newer-model car came into view, riding the center line for a heart-beat before drifting back. The radar squealed, a rising tone that snapped my eyes to the display.

Thirty over.

For a second I blinked, half-sure fatigue was trying to trick me.

Hazard lights flashed through the dark like a warning all their own.

Most people don't run hazards when they're joyriding or drunk, I thought.

I swung the cruiser around, light bar still dark, closing the distance. The car held steady—no swerving, no panic, no overcorrection. Just speed. Anxious. Deliberate.

I lit him up.

Blue light washed across the back glass. The siren shattered the night. The car slowed immediately, pulling to the shoulder without drama. No delay. No wobble. A clean, controlled stop.

I called it in and stepped out into the crisp air.

The driver's window was already down. Single male, mid-thirties, hands visible on the wheel. His face was wet, eyes red—not from alcohol, but from something heavier.

"Evening," I said, keeping my tone level. "Do you know why I stopped you?"

"I'm sorry," he blurted, the word breaking loose before anything else. "I'm sorry. I know I was speeding."

Crying—not angry, not defiant. The kind that arrives before a man can organize his thoughts.

"License and registration," I said. "Tell me what's going on."

He fumbled his wallet, nearly dropping it, then handed everything to me like the moment might collapse if he hesitated.

"My father," he said, breath hitching. "My dad's in the hospital. Car wreck. They called me. They said—"

He stopped and swallowed hard.

"They said I need to get there. They called the family in."

That last part settled between us, heavier than the strip of asphalt we stood on.

The hazards clicked steadily beside us, a soft metronome. I leaned in just enough to read him. No alcohol. No slur. No fogged stare. Just a man in free fall at three in the morning.

"Which hospital?" I asked.

"Fifteen minutes," he said. "Maybe ten if—"

He caught himself.

I looked at his license, then back at him again. Thirty over is the kind of stop that pads numbers—one of those catches supervisors like to see written cleanly in a report.

But this man wasn't a number.

He was someone's son trying to outrun a phone call.

Top's voice drifted through memory—quiet, steady: Everyone carries something you can't see. Your job is to decide whether the law helps—or crushes them with it.

He looked up at me, bracing.

"You were speeding," I said. "You know that. But your driving was controlled. Hazards on. No weaving. You're not trying to beat the clock—you're trying to get to your father."

His chin trembled. He nodded once.

"Here's what we're going to do," I said. "You're going to take a breath. You're going to drive the rest of the way like his life depends on you getting there safe—not faster. Understand?"

He covered his mouth, shoulders shaking. "Yes, sir. Thank you."

"I'm sorry about your father," I said. And I meant it. "Go be with your family."

He eased the car into gear, almost afraid I'd change my mind, then pulled back onto the highway. Hazards blinking. Speed steady. Taillights shrinking until the dark took them back.

I stood there a moment longer, listening as the night folded in again. I said a quiet prayer, then cleared the stop and finished the shift.

Before heading home, I called the hospital. I didn't have to. I needed to know.

It didn't take long.

A nurse confirmed that his father had died shortly after arrival.

I stared at the screen under the cold fluorescent hum, feeling that familiar mix of sadness and something steadier. Sadness for him. Relief that—for once—the system hadn't placed itself between a man and a goodbye.

Later that morning, the Chief stepped into the report room, a folder in his hand. He glanced at the narrative, then at me.

"This your stop?" he asked.

"Yes, sir."

He read it once more, closed the folder, and set it down.

"You made the right call," he said.

No lecture. No qualifier. Just that.

By the time the sky began to pale, the weight of the night was still riding with me—not heavy, but present. A reminder that discretion isn't the absence of law.

Sometimes it's the point of it.

At three in the morning on a quiet Carolina highway, I let a man go.

I've carried that decision with me ever since.

Reflections in the Rearview

By dawn of my last night shift that week, the town had softened around the edges.

Fog off the sound drifted between buildings like it had lost its way, turning the streetlights into smudges of gold. The sky was still bruised with the last shades of night, but a narrow line of cobalt pressed along the horizon—steady, patient, indifferent to whatever the darkness had taken. Somewhere downtown, a bakery had already begun its morning rhythm. Warm bread and yeast threaded through the cruiser's vents, settling over the end of a long week like a quiet reminder that not everything in the world was hard.

It was the first gentle thing I'd felt in hours.

Shifts don't end with final calls; they end when the town exhales. That slow unwinding always hit hardest at the week's close—when the adrenaline had drained away, the paperwork was stacked and done, and your body carried the faint echoes of every room, every voice, every choice you'd stepped into. The quiet wasn't peace. It was the aftermath.

I pulled into the station lot just as first shift drifted in. The tired nods officers gave each other at this hour were stripped of bravado—small acknowledgments between people who'd fought their battles in different corners of the same night. You could tell who'd had a heavy shift by the looseness of their belts, the way they lingered at their trunks, and the slump in their shoulders before stepping inside.

Inside, the squad room was too bright. Fluorescents flickered overhead like they resented being awake. Someone laughed—sharp, sudden, too loud—and a few others joined in. It wasn't about the joke. It never was. That kind of laughter is armor, a way to keep the night from climbing into your head and staying there.

The coffee tasted burnt and metallic. The linoleum looked the same—scuffed, tired, and unbothered by whatever the dark had demanded. Reports sat half-folded on desks, waiting for signatures from people already imagining the moment their boots came off. The room hadn't changed.

But I had.

I slid my reports into the tray and sat for a moment, letting the hum of the building settle around me. The wall clock ticked a fraction off-tempo, each click a reminder that time didn't care what you'd witnessed—only that you kept moving. The badge on my chest felt heavier—not the metal, but what I now understood it carried.

I caught my reflection in the glass of the trophy case, past the confiscated guns and knives displayed like the town's old sins under fluorescent light. My uniform was dirty from the seatbelt. A faint smear of dust streaked my cheek—from the Blackbeard house, or the restaurant kitchen, or the domestic. Hard to tell anymore. The rookie I'd been was still there some-where, but he looked smaller now—set back behind the eyes of someone who'd learned to stand still when chaos tried to take the lead.

Someone who no longer waited for permission.

Someone who had begun to understand the cost.

Someone stepping into a space Top once said existed, though I hadn't believed him then.

The door opened, and Top stepped into the squad room. For a heartbeat, the air tightened the way it always did—no easing, just a room remembering its posture.

He didn't say a word. He didn't need to. He lifted his chin once—slow, deliberate.

Approval. Recognition. A quiet passing of something earned.

I returned the nod. It lasted a second—maybe less—but it settled deeper than any commendation could.

He walked past, boots echoing down the hall until the sound folded back into the building's steady hum. I watched him go, realizing that—for the first time since stepping into this job—I wasn't trying to match his stride.

For the first time, I wasn't chasing his shadow.

I was standing on my own.

And I had no idea yet how dark it would get in the chapters ahead—or how much that shadow would matter.

Aftermath

Standing on your own doesn't make the weight any lighter when a week finally breaks. After a stretch like that one, you expect the last shift to end in relief. It never does. The end of the night just smudges into the begin-ning of something heavier, and morning doesn't feel like an ending—it feels like an echo.

I drove home as the sky began to pale, the roads empty except for delivery trucks, newspaper carriers, and a few early joggers pretending not to notice the cruiser easing past. Dawn always makes the town look innocent, as if the darkness never happened. Windows warmed with kitchen lights. Coffee dripped in quiet houses. No one knew what the night took—or what we carried out of it.

When I stepped out of the car, the chill hit harder than it should have. My thoughts drifted back to the man who lost his father. The man trapped in a lonely house. The smell of spilled beer that followed me no matter how long I'd driven with the windows down.

Inside my house, the silence felt foreign. No radio static. No calls for a status check. Just the hum of the fireplace fan and the soft tick of a wall clock marking a world untouched by the night. The contrast was jarring—like stepping out of a storm and realizing the rest of the world stayed dry.

I hung my jacket on the hook behind the door and paused. The badge caught a shard of morning light and flashed once. A long breath left me—one I hadn't realized I'd been holding.

Sleep came in fragments. Dispatch tones. Creaking floorboards. Doors opening and closing. Not nightmares—just the mind trying to file away what didn't fit anywhere.

I woke before noon with my heartbeat still uneven. The job hadn't let go yet. The job leaves a residue you can't scrub off.

Outside, dawn broke clean over the sound, light spilling through the curtains like forgiveness. The town exhaled. I did too. But the quiet never lasts long in this job. It isn't peace. It's the breath before the next lesson.

That evening, when I walked back into the squad room—boots on linoleum, radios crackling, someone cursing at the coffee filter—the weight shifted. The quiet slipped off my shoulders. Familiar noise steadied me in a way rest never could.

You can face the dead alone.

But you return to the living with the ones who understand what that costs.

Before the next shift was done, they proved it—not with speeches or ceremony, but with headlights swinging through the dark and cruisers sliding in from every direction. Doors slammed. Leather creaked. Radios murmured low at the edge of a silence that always forms when trouble waits behind a wall.

On paper, we were just a shift.

Standing there under buzzing lights, watching those units stack up one by one, something settled in my bones. When one of us says, "I need another unit," what we're really saying is this: "Don't let me stand in this storm alone."

And they never did.

Some lessons take a week to learn. Others arrive in a single voice on the radio.

* * *

There's a point early in every officer's career when the job stops feeling like a test and starts feeling like a shared weight. It doesn't happen all at once. It builds—call by call, night by night—until you realize the strength you thought you were carrying alone has been held up by others the whole time.

I didn't understand that at the academy.

I didn't fully understand it during my first solo week.

But the night that followed made it undeniable.

Brotherhood isn't announced.

It doesn't need words.

It shows up—quiet, uninvited—when the dark tightens and a single voice hits the radio asking for help.

Chapter 4—Brotherhood in Blue

The things ordained for you—teach yourself to be at one with those.
And the people who share them with you—treat them with love.
With real love.

—Marcus Aurelius

Every officer learns that survival isn't just a learned skill—it's reliance. It's depending on others. You might drive alone, but you never really do this job by yourself. You learn that early in the squad room—in the bad coffee, the laughter that shouldn't be funny but is, the way jokes land sharper at three in the morning because everyone understands what they're pushing back against. What holds you together isn't ceremony; it's proximity. It's being around people who know what the night can take out of you, even when you don't yet have language for it.

By the end of my first week solo, that understanding had weight. I'd faced the dead, the violent, the desperate, and the moments afterward that were somehow harder. And when the silence got too heavy, I found myself steering back toward the station—toward the room, the noise, and the familiar faces that steadied the space just by being there. Sometimes it was nothing more than a glance and a nod as you walked in, or a joke drifting across the linoleum at exactly the right moment. Small things that kept you standing without anyone naming why.

You don't go there looking for comfort—you go because the job strips you thin in ways you didn't know could tear, and you need one place where you can set your duty belt down without explaining yourself. The only people who understand that kind of wear are the ones carrying it too. Some nights, laughter did the work—too loud, too sharp, thrown like a rope before the next call pulled us under. Other nights, it was the stillness between us, easy and unforced. Cops are proud. We learn early how to keep things masked.

The academy taught me how to survive a call. The job taught me where to go once it was over.

Threaded through all of it was a truth I was only beginning to understand: skill might keep you alive in the moment, but it's the people beside you who help you stand once the moment passes. Top used to say we depend on each other more than we realize—not just in the fight, but afterward, when the adrenaline drains and what's left has to be carried somewhere.

I didn't know it yet, but the nights ahead would show me exactly where that reliance lived—and how much of myself I'd end up trusting to it.

Roll Call

The shifts always began the same way—half-awake cops gathered under the hum of fluorescent lights, clutching burnt coffee like medicine. The sergeant read through the previous shift's calls in a voice that sounded older than the room. The air held that familiar mix of leather, starch, and cheap cologne—the smell that seemed to follow every police building I'd ever stepped into.

Nicknames flew fast. The guy who once dumped chili down his uniform was forever "Bean." A rookie who froze on his first traffic stop became "Statue." You didn't choose your name; the squad chose it for you, and it sometimes stuck longer than your badge number.

And me?

After the night I walked a naked, furious woman out of an apartment and into the magistrate's office, the squad tried out half a dozen names—"Streaker," "Birthday Suit," even "Clothing Optional."

Thankfully none of them stuck—but the laughter did.

Once the clipboard closed and the doors opened, the room shifted. The joking thinned, keys were checked, and radios were clipped back into place. Whatever waited outside would meet us as individuals, but it never felt that way when we stood there together, coffee cups cooling in our hands.

Some of that steadiness came from the people beside you—the ones who'd sit shoulder to shoulder in a cruiser and say nothing because nothing needed saying. And some of it came from voices you never saw.

What happened in the squad room was only half of it. The other half lived behind glass, in a room most citizens would never enter. Dispatchers heard everything—fear, anger, confusion—without ever stepping into the scene. I used to wonder how they carried it.

You could tell who was working the radio by the way they spoke. Some voices were crisp and direct. Others carried a warmth you felt even through the static.

Either way, when they spoke, the noise settled.

I remember one pursuit out past the town line.

The radio turned chaotic—sirens, stepped-on transmissions, and units calling at once. Then a single calm voice cut through it all.

"Units in pursuit, all traffic hold."

Just like that, everything slowed. Lanes cleared. Breathing followed.

Someone behind the microphone had the reins.

After that night, roll call didn't feel like a routine anymore. It felt like alignment—everyone taking their place before the town decided what kind of night it would be. We worked from different sides of the building—a gun and badge in the car, a keyboard and mic in the comms room—but when things started to tilt toward panic, it was another human voice that brought you back to center.

Roll call ended the same way every night—with the uneasy sense that the next call could land anywhere between comedy and catastrophe.

And when the room emptied and the radios came alive again, that sense went with you. Into the cruiser. Into the first call. Into the spaces between calls, when the tension had to go somewhere before it turned inward.

Pranks and Rituals

We weren't held together by speeches. It was built in smaller ways—inside jokes whispered over radio static, nicknames earned in embarrassment, laughter spilling down hallways when the rest of the world slept. The town had its rhythms—sirens, heartbreak, noise—but ours ran on stranger fuel.

One night, after clearing a call near a convenience store by a homeless camp, a couple of the guys slipped around back and started letting out moans worthy of a horror flick—deep, guttural, half-human sounds that drifted out of the dark. I nearly dropped my flashlight. My hand went straight for the holster before the laughter hit—sharp and uncontrolled, bouncing off brick walls until even I was laughing too. No one admitted it, but we all needed that release. Real screams came often enough. Sometimes you had to fake one just to remember what it felt like to laugh before the next real one found you.

Meals became their own ritual. The public thought cops lived on donuts. The truth was we lived in diners—late-night booths, burnt coffee, eggs that tasted faintly like the pan, and the quiet comfort of sitting with your back to the wall so you could watch the door. We learned to eat fast, talk faster, and never order anything you couldn't box up in ten seconds when the radio crackled. Still, for that hour wedged between calls, those booths felt steady—ordinary in a job that rarely was.

*　*　*

One holiday, we broke the routine and decided to grill steaks at the station.

We pooled our cash, raided the grocery store, and came back loaded with meat and flimsy paper plates. I thought it was just dinner. It wasn't.

The sergeant and corporal had a plan. The corporal—a hulking SWAT vet with a wicked grin and a love for mischief—parked his cruiser near the entrance, its dashcam conveniently aimed toward the grill. While the rest of us chopped onions and swapped stories, he slipped outside and set the trap: two M-80s tucked under the lid and a half-shredded K-9 possum chew toy wedged inside.

An hour later, the steaks were marinating, and someone called out, "Hey, did anyone check the propane?"

Our unlucky volunteer—a veteran with an unlit cigar clamped between his teeth and more confidence than caution—strolled out to the patio, muttering about how he was the "pit master."

Seconds later, the corporal burst into the squad room, tears streaming down his face, VHS tape in hand. "You've got to see this," he wheezed.

We crowded around the ancient TV. Static, then grainy footage: the officer, the grill, the lift of the lid—boom. The M-80s cracked, the toy squealed, and he shot straight up like a rocket—arms pinwheeling, cigar gone mid-air. He landed running, pure cartoon physics brought to life.

"He should've shot the possum," I said, trying to sound braver than I felt. Truth was, any one of us would've jumped—we just hoped the camera never caught us doing it.

* * *

The job wore you down one shift at a time. The ridiculous moments—the fake ghosts, the exploding grill, the nicknames, the late-night diners—kept you from carrying all of it at once. Laughter didn't fix anything. It just loosened the grip long enough to keep moving.

And when the room finally went quiet again, it happened fast. Chairs scraped back. Belts were checked. Someone reached for their keys.

The radio cracked to life.

We were already moving.

The Attic Call

We might as well have had Animal Control stitched across our uniforms.

If there was a call about something hissing, howling, scratching, or slithering, it somehow landed with us.

That night, dispatch sent us to a report of "something moving in the attic."

When we arrived, an older woman met us at the door—gray hair pinned tight, housecoat buttoned to the neck. She smelled faintly of cinnamon. The house was an old Victorian in the historic district, the kind that creaked even when it was trying to stay quiet. Moonlight pressed through lace curtains, turning the hallway pale and thin.

She whispered like the walls were listening.

"It's been scratching for days," she said. "Right above my bedroom. Something's up there."

My partner grinned. "Probably a squirrel."

"Or a possum," I said.

"Or a ghost," he offered, half serious, half joking.

We argued about who was going up. A coin toss settled it.

I lost.

The pull-down ladder groaned like it had opinions about my weight. I'd cleared basements, crawl spaces, and even a junkyard once—but attics were their own kind of haunted. The air up there had a memory. It was cold and stale, too still, like the world had stopped breathing years ago.

My flashlight cut through the dust, turning it into slow-moving snow. For a while, there was nothing. Then a faint sound—a soft whimper, followed by another.

I froze.

"Something's up here," I called down, voice tight, hand resting on the butt of my gun.

My partner's voice floated back.

"If it's the ghost, tell her to keep it down. Day shift's sleeping."

I edged closer, the beam sweeping over trunks, cobwebs, and forgotten furniture. Another whimper—tiny and uneven. My chest tightened. I aimed the light toward the sound and saw movement—a flicker, then stillness.

Then I saw them.

Three masked bandits, huddled together in a torn quilt, eyes glinting like marbles in the light. Small. Perfectly alive.

No mother in sight. No threat. Just intruders too young to know they'd been caught.

Relief hit like a laugh I didn't quite let out. I climbed down and told the homeowner. She gasped, placing a hand over her chest.

"Oh, Lord," she said. "I imagined it was something much worse."

We called the local wildlife rescue. While we waited, we found the entry point—a warped section of siding under the eaves where the mother had probably slipped through.

When the rescue team arrived, they coaxed the babies into a small carrier. The homeowner exhaled like she'd been holding her breath for a week. She promised to have her son repair the siding in the morning.

I smiled.

"Make sure you call us before your son goes into the attic," I said.

"Day shift will love this!" I thought.

As we packed up, my partner muttered, "At least it wasn't a ghost."

I nodded. "Not tonight."

And as we stepped off that creaking porch, I realized the job wasn't always about the worst moments people imagined. Sometimes it was about the quiet calls—the ones that ended with a locked attic and fear draining away instead of deepening.

That calm never lasted.

As we wiped attic dust from our boots and keyed the mic back on, the radio crackled to life again—sharp, urgent, familiar. Somewhere else in town, someone was already screaming.

We turned the cruiser toward it and drove.

Fights and Near-Misses

The station still smelled faintly of cigar smoke and steak grease when the radio reminded us why laughter never lasted long. No matter how good the prank or how loud the joking, the radio always cut through it—pulling us from nonsense back into the knowledge that the next voice crackling through the static might drag us straight into a fight we might not walk away from.

I was partnered with one of our veterans—a female officer with fifteen years on the job, built like grit wrapped in muscle and a smile. The kind of cop who didn't flinch, didn't crack, and didn't let you down. She wasn't someone you wanted to scrap with in a bar, let alone in a hallway with no exits.

The call was a domestic in the projects. The name the dispatcher read was familiar, the kind that carried its own weight in the room. Everyone had arrested him at least once. Some twice. A few more times than that.

When we pulled up, his girlfriend met us on the porch. Her face was bloody, with several teeth missing and another chipped. Rage twisted her features almost as much as the pain.

"I want him arrested," she snapped. "My teeth are broken. Who's gonna pay for it?"

Inside, the apartment smelled like stale beer soaked into carpet, fried food clinging to the air, and the tang of old cigarettes baked into the walls. The TV was still on—a boxing match playing to no one. The whole place felt like a punch waiting to land.

He was in the back bedroom, sprawled across the bed like a king on a throne made of dirty laundry. One beer nearly empty in his hand, another cracked open on the nightstand. He looked at us with calm resignation—no remorse, no fear, just a drunk man who knew the script.

"Put the beer down," I said. Once. Twice.

He didn't.

I reached for the can, and that was all it took. He lunged, and gravity did the rest—we hit the floor with a thud that rattled the dresser. I ended up on top, fighting to keep his hands pinned as he bucked beneath me, yelling, "All I wanna do is finish my damn beer!" Foam sprayed across the carpet, soaking into my sleeves.

My partner dropped beside me, trying to grab his other wrist. She'd been through thousands of fights; this was routine for her—until the girlfriend snapped.

And it was instant—something broke in her eyes, a hurt turning into fury so fast it didn't have time to warn her own body what it was doing. She lunged at my partner, shrieking, nails flashing, hair wild. "Get off my boyfriend!" she screamed, voice cracking. In her hand—scissors. Long and sharp, glinting under the bare bulb.

She brought them down.

The blade hit my partner's vest with a dull punch, slowed by Kevlar but still driving home hard enough to steal her breath. She hissed through clenched teeth but didn't let go of his wrist.

The girlfriend froze for half a heartbeat—realizing what she'd just done—then bolted.

But he was still thrashing under me, drunk strength mixed with stubborn pride. We dragged him down first, forcing the cuffs on while adrenaline blurred the edges of everything else. My hands shook once the fight settled—nothing visible, just that deep tremor you feel in your bones after your body realizes it survived something your mind hasn't caught up with.

Only when he was secure did I chase her—catching her just before she reached the kitchen door, pinning her wrists as she screamed and twisted like a feral thing.

He just lay there smirking, drunk and satisfied, like finishing that beer had been worth every busted tooth and every felony.

Later, as ambulance lights washed the walls in red, I kept hearing her voice—"My teeth are broken"—echoing against the memory of her screams as she tried to stab the woman who'd come to help her.

That was the truth of domestics: betrayal stacked on violence, victims turning into attackers without warning, and the ground dropping out from under you before you even knew it moved.

And it carved something permanent in me—a truth every cop learns sooner or later.

Survival isn't just strength or training.

It's the partner beside you—bleeding, battered, but refusing to break.

That was the job in its purest form: someone stepping into the swing meant for you. It wasn't a slogan. It was a dent in a vest and a bruise that should have been yours.

The call was over, but the lesson stayed: in this job, the line between living and not living was often just the reach of a partner's hand.

The Call That Changed How I Saw Brotherhood

My first real taste of brotherhood didn't come during roll call or over coffee. It came on a hot summer night, standing outside a row of familiar apartments where the air smelled of sweat, smoke, and stale beer.

I'd been dispatched to a loud music complaint at one of our local hotspots—the kind of neighborhood you didn't drive into without a few cruisers behind you. A small crowd was gathered around a burn barrel, flames licking at scraps of wood, music thumping through the thin apartment walls.

When I pulled up, most of them scattered inside. The music kept pounding. I knocked on the nearest door, just planning to ask them to turn it down. The door cracked open—then a boot caught me square in the chest. I stumbled back as the door slammed. I thought about my BLET training and Top's lessons and realized I'd broken nearly every rule I'd been taught. Tactical awareness, always.

"Never stand in front of a door," I heard the voice in my head—calm, certain, like he was still there watching me make the mistake. The kick bruised more than my ribs. It bruised my pride—and pride, left unchecked, can get a cop killed faster than any blade.

Once backup officers arrived, I only wanted the one who kicked me.

The apartment was small and stifling, with shadows moving behind torn curtains and furniture. People were hiding everywhere—under mattresses, behind doors, and in closets. Knives flashed in their hands. Fear makes people reach for steel. I wasn't there for them. I just wanted the one who'd assaulted me.

I stepped into the kitchen and froze. That's when I saw her. I recognized her—the streetwalker who drifted in and out of our nights like a shadow. She was crouched behind the counter. A butcher knife pressed against her chest, eyes darting.

"Drop the knife," I said.

Nothing.

I drew my pepper spray and leaned around the corner. The mist hit the air—and she came out swinging. The blade caught my arm, shallow but sharp, before she dropped it. I unholstered my weapon, and for a second, we just stared—her wide-eyed, me steady, waiting.

For one beat, I knew I might have to shoot her.

Then she dropped the knife and started to cry. I holstered the gun and moved in to cuff her, but she twisted and fought, forgetting the line she'd almost crossed. Blood from my arm soaked into my sleeve.

But what I remember most isn't the pain. It's the sound of boots. Two officers hit the kitchen hard, dragging me clear while another took the woman down. I was still new, still earning my place. But at that moment, none of it mattered. The badge on my chest was enough.

Outside, the air felt cooler, cleaner, unreal—like the world had kept turning while we'd been fighting to stay in it.

Later, in the ER, one of them leaned against the curtain, uniform still streaked with sweat and dust. He smirked.

"You'll get used to it," he said. "We all bleed for each other."

Then he tossed me a candy bar from the vending machine.

I lay there staring at the ceiling, arm burning, ribs aching, listening to the steady beep of the monitor. All I wanted to do was take a shower and wash the night off of me.

Somewhere down the hall, a stretcher rattled past. Someone laughed. Someone cursed.

And I understood it then—not as an idea, but as a fact.

When things went bad, you weren't alone.

Someone was already moving toward you.

Medic on Midnights

They call EMS when the bleeding starts and when it finally stops. On midnights, I learned that the room belongs to whoever can steady it first. Most nights, that was me until the medics arrived. People don't notice that handoff. I do.

I was running radar on the highway shoulder when dispatch called: "Check in with EMS." It didn't sound urgent—just one of those quick welfare checks we made a habit of. The least we could do was roll by and wait for the thumbs-up that everything was fine.

When I turned down the side street, the EMS rig sat crooked in a driveway, rear doors open, lights pulsing soft red against the siding. At first glance nothing looked off—then I heard shouting. The kind that cuts through engine noise.

A male medic came into view, dragging a man out the front door and shoving him into the yard. The man stumbled, spun, and squared his shoulders like he meant to go back in. I was already out of the patrol car before he found his balance. He swung once—clumsy, slowed by alcohol—and I took him down into the grass, cuffs clicking tight before he could get another word out.

The air stank of beer and sweat. Somewhere inside, a radio buzzed with half-finished medical codes. I walked him to the cruiser, placed him in the back seat, and cracked the window. The smell of alcohol filled the cab—thick, sour, clinging to the vinyl. Night air crawled in—diesel and a hint of rain on asphalt. The usual Carolina mix of calm and corrosion.

When I stepped back inside, the scene was still settling. A female medic sat on the couch, an ice pack pressed to her face, blood bright under one eye. She'd been hit mid-call, caught between helping and defending herself. Her partner hovered nearby, voice low, hands steady, keeping the room from tipping again.

She looked up when she saw me and nodded once. "I'm okay," she said.

I nodded back. We both knew she wasn't.

The medics packed their bags slowly, moving with the kind of focus that comes after chaos. One of them paused long enough to say, "Thanks for the timing."

I told him it was nothing. It wasn't. It never is.

Later, back in the rig bay, another crew member mentioned my hands had been shaking a little. Maybe they were. What mattered was that I kept breathing. That's the measure—it's never whether you shake, only whether you keep breathing through it.

*   *   *

A few weeks later, the same medic crew and I crossed paths again on a code in the median—opioid overdose, skin the color of paper. I threw the cruiser sideways and became a lighthouse with a light bar, moving traffic with my body because that's what the scene needed. They worked compressions so hard I felt the rhythm in my own shoulders.

When they got a pulse and the rig doors slammed, I stepped back into the dark, reopened lanes, and let the town swallow us both.

On nights like that, it wasn't the uniform that steadied things—it was whoever arrived ready to work. Sometimes that was me. Sometimes it was them. Control passed hand to hand without ceremony, the way it always does when people know their roles.

I watched them load gear, check straps, and climb back into the rig. The doors shut. The engine turned over. Red lights washed the median once more—then disappeared down the road.

I got back in my cruiser, keyed the mic, and waited.

Another call was already lining up.

The Family You Don't Choose

People always assumed cops were hardened by the job—armor first, emotions last. But the truth was simpler: we became a family, not by blood or upbringing, but by choosing the same path when everyone else turned away. That loyalty didn't arrive all at once. It grew slowly, in the everyday rituals that held us together long before the night tried to pry us apart.

We celebrated everything—promotions, weddings, first apartments, the birth of a child, and even the first time someone managed to cook a steak without turning it into charcoal. If someone brought in a baby, the squad room transformed instantly. Officers with forearms like railroad ties cradled an eight-pound newborn as if it were made of glass. Someone always joked the kid looked like Top. For a few minutes, the world outside didn't exist.

Real families sometimes miss these things. We didn't know childhood stories, but we knew who flinched at sudden noises, who hated basements and spiders, and who laughed too loud when they were scared. We knew whose back still ached from a fight last weekend and whose marriage was hanging on by one thin thread. We learned each other the way soldiers learn ground—by surviving the same nights.

When someone new arrived—a rookie still stiff in a pressed uniform, eyes wide, trying not to show it—we brought them in on purpose. A chair got pulled out. Space was made. The unwritten rules were handed over quietly. Not to haze them. Not to test them. Just to make sure they knew they weren't stepping into the dark alone. It usually started small—someone catching their eye across the room, leaning back in a chair, asking, You good?

It wasn't a question people asked casually. Most folks didn't see the ghosts riding along or the weight that stayed after the radio went quiet. They didn't see what followed you home or how close some nights still felt long after the call cleared. We understood that if we didn't look out for each other, no one else would. So when someone asked, You good? It wasn't small talk or politeness—it was a check of the gauge, a way of seeing how much was left in the tank, whether someone was still steady or starting to slip.

Birthdays were chaos. Someone bought the wrong cake, someone forgot plates, and someone always lit too many candles, convinced the fire code didn't apply if the birthday boy was the one writing the report. Once, a corporal filled the patrol sergeant's car with fake spiders, from floorboard to dash, after the sergeant admitted he hated spiders. He pretended to be furious. Later, we caught him trying on the spider rings.

Holidays carried their own rituals. If you worked Christmas, someone's spouse delivered enough food to feed a platoon. On Thanksgiving, crockpots appeared—barbecue, vegetable soup, and chili strong enough to stun a horse. Paper plates. Flickering fluorescents. Laughter at jokes that would have ended our careers anywhere else. Someone always said grace—half sincere, half sarcastic—but it worked. It made the shift feel less like a burden and more like a gathering.

Some nights, even after a shift ended, people stayed because going home felt too quiet. The squad room filled that silence. Shoulder to shoulder on battered couches, stories moved back and forth—some funny, some brutal—until the air felt lighter. There was no official therapy in that room.

But there was healing. Someone would ask it softly, almost offhand, the way they always did—You good?" And sometimes the answer mattered less than knowing the question was still being asked.

We weren't blood. We didn't need to be. What held us together was forged in shared meals, stupid pranks, and the quiet certainty that someone would answer when the radio screamed. The badge didn't make us family. The life did.

For a long time, that was enough—until the first night it wasn't, and we had to learn what brotherhood meant when even our best couldn't hold someone here.

Still, not every reminder of who we were came wrapped in darkness. Some arrived in daylight, when the radio stayed quiet and the job asked something different of us. A street closed for laughter instead of sirens. A gym filled with kids instead of tension. Moments that reminded us we weren't only responding to a community—we belonged to it.

We were part of the same streets we drove through every night.

And nothing showed that more clearly than the times we took the badge into the open—not to stop trouble, but to stand beside the people we served and give something back.

Cops for Kids

We didn't know if it would work.

It was our department's first year trying Cops for Kids, and we'd hustled hard—local donations, bake sales, officers slipping cash from their own wallets. When we finally counted it all, we had enough to bring fifteen kids shopping.

Inside the store, kids darted between aisles, bright lights flashing off garland and ornaments. Officers pushed carts like they were navigating a slow-motion parade, radios clipped to jackets, duty belts creaking against plastic handles.

My assigned trio—Mia (15), Jaden (10), and Kira (8)—stood close together, like one heartbeat. My wife walked beside me, and our youngest son took charge of "helping," which mostly meant steering the cart into displays.

While most kids sprinted toward toys, Mia led us straight to clothes.

A new coat for Kira.

Shoes for Jaden.

Winter basics.

The money went fast. My sergeant drifted by and slipped a gift card into my hand without making eye contact.

"For whatever they won't pick for themselves," he said.

When we reached the toy aisles, Jaden practically vibrated. Kira found a glittery backpack that lit up. But Mia stayed back, watching quietly.

My wife stepped beside her.

"What do you want?"

Mia shrugged. "Maybe some makeup. Maybe clothes."

"Push a second cart," my wife said gently. "Tonight's for you, too."

Something in the girl broke open. Her breath caught, tears rising before she even reached for the handle.

We filled the cart slowly—makeup, jeans, a warm sweater, boots. She handled each item carefully, like it might disappear if she moved too fast.

At checkout, my wife drifted to another lane, paid for the entire second cart with her own money, and returned without saying a word.

When she handed the bags to Mia, the girl collapsed into her arms, crying hard enough to shake both of them. My wife cried too—quiet at first, then without trying to stop it.

Outside, kids ran through the glow of cruiser lights, breath puffing white in the cold. Officers laughed alongside them, hands in pockets, radios finally quiet.

My son tugged my sleeve.

"Dad," he said, "can we do this again?"

Standing there in the wash of fluorescent lights and Christmas music, I knew exactly what he meant.

Blessing and Burden

What tied us together wasn't history or familiarity—it was proximity to the same nights and the same risks. You learned quickly who would show up, who stayed calm when things tipped sideways, and who didn't need to announce it. That kind of reliance didn't arrive all at once. It revealed itself slowly, in how people moved, where they stood, and what they did when the moment demanded more than words.

The same men who tackled suspects also absorbed each other's damage. You carried the grief of a widow, the guilt of a split-second mistake, and the images that woke your partner at three in the morning. Support wasn't something you scheduled or requested—it was simply there, assumed. The weight got shared quietly, parceled out in small ways, because naming it didn't make it any lighter.

From the outside, the badge looked like authority. From the inside, it felt like responsibility layered on responsibility—serious, relentless, and occasionally absurd. You were expected to hold the line when it mattered and take the jokes when you didn't. Both were part of the deal.

*   *   *

The shift had ended fifteen minutes earlier. My car was already running, and sunrise was stretching cobalt across the water. I was ready to go home when dispatch called: an issue on the beach near one of the turtle mounds.

A few weeks before, a loggerhead had wandered onto the road, drawn by streetlights, and been hit by a car. It had landed heavier on us than we ever admitted. So when this call came in, I went.

I walked up the beach access and found the caller pointing at the dunes like he'd stumbled onto a crime scene. A snake had curled itself across a turtle nest and decided to wait there for breakfast.

I radioed in the update and grabbed my snake tongs and the shotgun loaded with snake shot. Calls like this were routine after spring—simple, quick, and uneventful.

At least, that's what I told myself.

By the time I reached the mound, twenty people had gathered like it was a beachside tailgate. I pushed them back and eased toward the snake. It coiled, tongue flicking, and tried to slip into a ghost-crab hole. I reached with the tongs, thinking I could trap it.

The moment the metal touched, it launched—striking, hissing, furious. I couldn't reach my shotgun, and my voice jumped two octaves when I called for backup.

My partner from the night before keyed his mic, siren wailing down the causeway.

"Hang tight, hero—I'm coming to save you," he laughed over the radio.

When he arrived, half the beach was watching. He made everyone step back, raised the shotgun, and fired. The snake fell still.

He turned toward me, grinning. "You good, Soprano?"

I never lived that one down. The guys played my radio clip over coffee—me yelping like a startled kid. Someone taped a plastic snake to my locker with a note that read, "Officer Safety Alert."

That was how it worked. You got roasted when you slipped and rescued when it counted.

It was a privilege to work beside people who would step into danger for you—and a burden to know that meant carrying their scars, their losses, and the stories that followed them home. Belonging came with a price, whether you asked for it or not.

Some nights, that truth showed up dressed as humor. Other nights, it arrived faster and louder, without warning. The difference was never whether someone showed up. It was how quickly they moved when it mattered.

As the crowd thinned and the beach settled back into quiet, we loaded gear and cleared the call. I keyed the mic, turned the cruiser toward the road, and pulled back into the stream of morning traffic.

The radio stayed quiet for a few miles.

Then it crackled again.

The Fire in His Garage

I'd known him for years.

The kind of officer everyone liked—the one who was always smiling, always first to lend a hand. If someone's dishwasher broke, he'd show up with a toolbox before you could even ask. If an officer couldn't afford the parts, he'd quietly cover it. The kind of man who'd give you the shirt off his back, even if it was the only one pressed clean.

He had recently remarried and was building his wife's dream house on a piece of land just outside town. Two kids—a boy and a girl—blond hair, barefoot summers, the kind of family that could've sat on a recruitment poster without trying.

Whenever we sat down after a shift, our conversations always drifted back to the same three things: God, family, and the work. Not in that order, and never forced. Faith wasn't something he performed or talked up—it was just there, steady, woven into how he saw the world. He believed policing gave his life purpose and that God had placed him exactly where he was supposed to be, badge and all.

He didn't say it like a sermon. He said it like a man who had settled the question for himself and moved on.

He had a few side hustles, like most cops did. He painted, mowed lawns, and worked construction—whatever it took to make ends meet.

"People don't become cops to get rich," he once said. "They do it because something in them wants to matter."

He was proof of that.

At first, nothing seemed off. He joked, he worked, and he volunteered for the shifts nobody wanted. Then small problems started showing— grumbles about how the house wasn't coming together fast enough, how he couldn't seem to make his wife happy no matter what he did. We all have those weeks, those nights when the job bleeds into home and the home feels heavier for it. Nobody thought it was more than that.

Then came the bombshell.

She was seeing someone else. She wanted a divorce.

He never said much about it—just brushed it off, like most cops are trained to do. Handle it. Move on. Don't let it show. But I could see something in his eyes shift, a dimming behind the easy grin. The way he laughed without meaning it. The way he stayed later at the station, cleaning out his cruiser long after the paperwork was done.

None of us saw the rest coming.

Not that day. Not that week.

The call came in before dinner: a fire at a new construction site on the west side. The address hit like a punch to the chest. It was his house.

By the time the units arrived, the garage was an inferno. Flames climbed the new frame, roaring through beams that still smelled of paint. The first on the scene said they knew before pulling the hose line—it wasn't just another fire.

He was inside the garage.

A single bullet. One decision that silenced everything he couldn't say.

The news spread fast, rolling through town like grief made visible. Nobody wanted to believe it. We told ourselves there had to be another explanation. But there wasn't. He'd been hurting, and we hadn't seen it—or maybe we had and didn't know how to reach him.

That's the part that stays.

Not the fire. Not the garage. The silence before it.

We thought he was happy. We thought he was fine. He probably thought he had no one to talk to. That's the curse of this work—we spend our lives listening to the broken but never learn how to speak for ourselves. We're trained to compartmentalize, to keep our armor polished and our wounds private.

And when the armor cracks, the stillness rushes in.

The day of the funeral, the procession stretched for miles.

Cruisers lined the highway shoulder to shoulder, lights flashing in synchronized grief. Strangers stood on overpasses holding flags. Kids stood in silence. No one judged him for how it ended. We only grieved that we hadn't found a way to stop it.

After the service, we stood by our cars longer than usual, talking about nothing—weather, schedules, football—because talking about him felt like admitting how fragile we all were.

Top's voice came back to me then, quiet as a whisper. "You can't always see the storm in someone else's sky. Sometimes all you can do is make sure they know they don't have to weather it alone. For us, that responsibility is real: encourage each other, build each other up, and don't mistake silence for strength."

I carried that with me.

That night, I drove past what was left of the house. The frame was gone, but the foundation remained, still warm under the headlights. I sat there with the engine idling, thinking about how a man can hold up an entire world for everyone else and never notice when it starts collapsing around him.

We tell ourselves the badge means strength.

But strength isn't silence.

It's noticing sooner.

It's reaching out before everything burns.

For a while afterward, the squad room felt subdued. Jokes landed softer. Check-ins stopped being small talk.

The job had begun to whisper what I hadn't yet learned to hear—that even brotherhood has ghosts. Some sit beside you in roll call. Some stand by your grave.

The Sergeant and Elvis

Not every night ended in grief or chaos. Sometimes the job swung hard in the opposite direction, dropping something so absurd it broke the tension entirely. Brotherhood lived there too—in the whiplash moments that pulled you back from the edge.

We'd just cleared a wreck and were heading back to the station to write reports when I rounded the curve in front of the station and slammed on the brakes.

The sergeant stood dead-center in the street, cruiser parked sideways like he'd staged his own traffic stop. Driver's door is wide open. Blue lights pulsing against the brick. And echoing down the empty road at full volume—Elvis Presley's "Hound Dog."

And there he was: hips shaking, arms swinging, sunglasses on at two in the morning, dancing like the King himself had been resurrected in uniform. He looked half ridiculous, half legendary—and entirely free.

That was him. Eccentric. Unapologetically joyful. The kind of leader who understood that if he didn't give us something to laugh at once in a while, the job would take too much out of us. Even on nights when a call hollowed you out, he'd catch your eye—not with a speech, not with a pat on the back, but with that look that meant, I get it. And you're going to be okay.

A few minutes later, a swarm of cruisers pulled in, each one slowing as the officers inside tried—and failed—to keep straight faces. Someone leaned out a window and started snapping their fingers. Someone else joined in with an off-key chorus. One of our toughest corporals tried to mimic Elvis's hip shake and nearly pulled something vital. The laughter that followed wasn't at him—it was with him. That distinction mattered.

Because in that laughter, just as much as in the silence of funerals or the chaos of fights, it lived. The job could take a lot from us—blood, sleep, years we didn't feel until they suddenly showed—but it couldn't take that.

Later, after report writing and the last checks, we didn't talk about the close calls or the mistakes or the things we'd carry home whether we meant to or not. We lingered in the parking lot, leaning against cruisers, watching the sunrise. No speeches. No thanks. Just proof we'd made it through another night.

As we finally drifted to our cars, the laughter thinning into quiet, something else settled in its place. A realization I couldn't yet name—that the badge carried more weight than pride alone could hold, and that brotherhood didn't just steady you. It reflected you back to yourself.

That morning, for the first time, I caught a glimpse of who I was becoming—not just a cop who'd survived another shift, but a man who would one day have to reckon with what all this belonging was costing him.

Chapter 5—The Mirror We Carry

It does not matter what you bear, but how you bear it.

—Seneca

The uniform changes more than how you look—it changes the room before you ever say a word. On the hanger, it's just leather, cloth, and metal. On the street, it becomes a story people tell themselves about you: hero, bully, savior, or problem. Some nights, that reflection feels like armor. Other nights, it looks back at you like an accusation, asking who you've become and whether you still recognize the person underneath.

When the Chief pinned the badge to my chest at graduation, I thought the job was simple. I'd taken the oath before, not realizing how often it would come back to test me. On paper, it was clean: protect, serve, defend. In reality, the oath wasn't just ink and ceremony—it was something sewn into the fabric of our lives and tested in alleys, living rooms, and at grave-side vigils. You didn't speak it once; you lived it a thousand small times or not at all.

Over time, the metal itself seemed to collect things. Every scream you couldn't unhear, every face you couldn't forget, every funeral you stood through in dress blues—they all settled there, pressed into that small piece of steel. Ghosts cling to the metal long before they show up in your dreams. Some nights I'd set it on the dresser, and it looked heavier there than it had on my chest, as if the stories it carried were finally allowed to sag.

What I didn't understand then was that the badge was more than a promise. It was a mirror.

It reflected whatever people needed it to be that day: reassurance in a grocery store when a child went missing or a painted target in a checkout line when someone saw only headlines. And sometimes it showed something harder—like the quiet shift in my child's eyes the first time he realized the world didn't see his parent the way he did. That look stayed with me long after the callouts faded.

And still, every morning, I pinned it back on—not because it was easy, or because the town loved us back in equal measure, but because someone had to wear the mirror and try to bear it well.

Before I could understand everything the badge was carrying, I had to understand what it looked like from the outside—how it shaped a room long before I ever spoke. And that lesson didn't come from a call or a mentor. It began with a single word, spoken in a hundred different tones, each one revealing who the world thought I was before I could say otherwise.

How the World Sees You

Before I ever learned what the badge meant to me, I had to learn what that one word meant to everyone who wasn't wearing it. Those lessons arrived in moments so ordinary I almost missed them—until they cut deeper than I expected.

The first time a child pointed at me and whispered, "police officer," the mirror was clean. Sharp, simple, and unclouded. I felt ten feet tall. His eyes were wide and unfiltered. For a heartbeat, I stood straighter, the metal catching the fluorescent light as if the job were simple: protector, helper, hero.

But I also remember the first time someone spat the same word. On a downtown sidewalk, a drunk hurled it like a curse across traffic. His anger wasn't at me, but at the uniform. That was the day I learned the badge carried more than steel. To some, it meant safety. To others, it meant enemy. And both could be true at once.

Not long after, I saw another version. One that still unsettles me. A mother leaned to her son in a grocery aisle and hissed, "You better behave or that policeman will take you away." His eyes snapped to mine, not with awe but with fear. In a single breath, the badge shifted from protector to threat. I wanted to kneel and tell him that it wasn't who we were, but the moment slipped. That's how fast a story can be written for you.

Moments like that reminded me the reflection wasn't just theirs—it was something I had to look into too.

The badge becomes whatever people need it to be—savior, oppressor, saint, scapegoat, or monster. Most days, the reflection chose me before I ever opened my mouth.

At home, the weight followed me inside. My parents looked at me with pride, but my mother's eyes carried a quiet thought she never said aloud: whether I would make it home tonight. Friends shifted, too. Conversations softened, jokes filtered. Even in familiar rooms, the uniform had a way of stepping through the door first. The badge was never invisible, even when I longed to be just another man in the room.

Once, a woman grabbed my arm in a department store, frantic after her child vanished down an aisle. She didn't care that I was off duty or that I had diapers and baby formula in my cart. She saw the badge, and to her it meant, Fix this now. We found her son hiding under a rack of coats, but the look she gave me afterward—a mix of relief and expectation—stayed with me. The badge wasn't permission. It was a responsibility.

And yet, it drew another kind of gaze—the ones that saw a target. I learned to sit facing the door in restaurants, not out of paranoia but pattern. You don't wear the badge without knowing it can paint a bullseye on your chest before you've spoken a word.

It was in the grocery store—off duty, jeans and a sweatshirt, my son in a stroller. The badge hung from a chain around my neck, more habit than need. We stood in line when a woman noticed it. Her eyes dropped, catching the shape of my gun tucked discreetly under my shirt. She gasped—sharp, loud, the kind of sound people make when they think they've just stumbled into danger. The fluorescent hum above us thickened, like the store itself was holding its breath.

In that instant, she wasn't looking at a father buying diapers. She was looking at a threat. Her whole expression changed—one moment she smiled at my son, the next she glared at me, muttering, "How dare he wear a gun," loud enough for every frozen-cart shopper around us to hear. As if I were the criminal who dared to be armed, forgetting I was a protector in disguise even on my off hours.

I wanted to explain. I wanted to tell her I wasn't the headline she'd read or the story she'd decided I fit into. I was just a dad running errands. But the badge didn't give me that choice. In her eyes, I wasn't a person anymore. I was the uniform.

My son tugged at my sleeve, confused, and asked why the lady was mad at me. I told him some people don't like police—and that was all I could manage.

The badge doesn't come off—not really. Even off duty, it walks in ahead of you.

That was the first time it felt heavy—not because of the metal, but because I realized it changed how the world looked at me and how my little boy looked at the world.

As he got older, he'd run to the door when I came home, tiny hands reaching for my duty belt before I could even unclip it. Later, he stopped asking about my night and started watching the news instead. One evening he switched off the TV and said, "I don't like when they talk about police." I told him not to worry, but I saw the fracture—the way his dad could be the hero in his world and the villain in someone else's.

That's when I understood it followed my family, too. The badge touches everyone under your roof, even the ones who never wear it.

We all swore the same oath once, standing stiff in pressed uniforms, right hands raised as silence pooled around us. I can still remember the dry paper smell and the soft click of dress shoes on tile. Never betray the badge, integrity, character, or public trust.

In reality, it was a vow proven in the quiet moments after danger passed—when the adrenaline drained and you were left alone with the truth of what you'd done. It was tested when a domestic victim turned on you mid-arrest. It was tested when you held fire because restraint was harder than pulling the trigger. It was tested when you stood in formation while bagpipes carried another officer into the ground. The oath wasn't spoken once. It was lived, again and again, or not at all.

But the heaviest burden isn't how others see you. It's what the badge absorbs: every call that clung to you, every scream that followed you home, every funeral that left its mark on your dress blues. On those nights, the badge felt heavier in memory than in metal. On the nights when weight found me, it felt like a shackle more than a shield. And yet, every morning, I pinned it back on.

Not because it was easy.

Not because I always wanted to.

Because someone had to.

On long nights I'd sit in the patrol car before roll call and watch the town wake up—store lights flicking on, people crossing streets with coffee in hand. They didn't see the badge, not really. They saw whatever story they carried: safety or suspicion, gratitude or fear. You learn to live inside that contradiction. You learn to serve a public that doesn't always want your help, to protect people who might curse your name tomorrow.

The badge puts you in a position to serve a town that doesn't always love you back—and you learn to do it anyway, because you remember the ones who still believe you're the good guy on the nights when the world stops believing in good guys at all.

We had each other.

What we couldn't control was who the world decided we were when we stepped out of the car.

The world could decide who I was in a grocery line or a parking lot, but identity gets tested in motion—in the noise, the heat, and the split-second moments where the badge stops being a symbol and becomes something you have to live up to. And nothing forces that reckoning faster than summer, when tempers run hot and the first real fight of the season is waiting for you just beyond the radio crackle.

Bar Fight

It was one of those early hot weekends of the year—the kind that pressed on you like a weight. We'd had stretches like this before: humidity clinging to the windows, the air thick enough to chew, the whole town simmering with the kind of restlessness that always showed up once the warm nights returned. Nothing big had happened in a while, and everyone on shift felt that uneasy energy that comes right before the season reminds you what it can turn into.

Dispatch came through at 00:47.

"Multiple subjects fighting at Crosswind Tavern. The bouncer is requesting police assistance. Possible stab wounds. Rescue standing by."

First big bar fight of the year.

They always came with heat and bad timing.

Crosswind Tavern sat on the edge of the county airport, a place where low-flying planes rattled the windows and the jukebox was older than half the patrons. When I turned into the gravel lot, silhouettes were already moving under the yellow wash of the parking-lot lights.

The bar's neon sign was dark. The bouncer had shut it down himself, afraid the brawl would destroy the business. But the crowd hadn't left. They'd spilled into the street—fifty people deep—voices sharp, laughter mean, fists twitching for something to do.

When they saw the cruiser, they didn't run.

They just stopped.

Turned toward the headlights as if deciding what to make of me.

For a second, I thought about how strange it was—how people can fight each other one minute, then join sides the next when a uniform rolls up.

The radio buzzed behind me: more units en route. Their sirens were distant—close enough to hope, too far to matter.

So it was me, for now.

I flipped on the blue lights and stepped out.

The heat hit like breath from a furnace—beer, sweat, asphalt, smoke. The air vibrated with tension, a low animal hum. Somewhere, a bottle clinked. Laughter followed, too loud, too forced.

Then the words came.

"Pigs."

"Pigs!"—the second one sharper, like they wanted it to stick.

"Honky!" someone spat.

"I got something for you!" barked a man near the front, his voice thick with drink and dare.

I could feel fifty pairs of eyes tracking me. The kind of stare that doesn't see a person—just the idea of one. My hand hovered near the radio mic, but I didn't key it. The crowd wasn't charging. Not yet. They were waiting to see who'd flinch first.

For a split second, adrenaline surged—the kind that spikes behind the ribs, cold and electric. I could feel every sound sharpen: the hum of the lights, the crunch of gravel under boots, the faint whine of a plane lifting somewhere beyond the fence, and the buzz of mosquitoes in the humid dark.

And then, like a clean cut through the noise, I heard Top's voice in my head.

"Don't take it personal. They don't see you—they see the badge. They see every headline, every rumor, every story they've ever been told. You can't carry all that. Just do the job right."

The words steadied my breathing and slowed the pulse hammering behind my chest. I raised my voice, even and low, not shouting—just cutting through.

"Alright," I said, calm but firm. "Bar's closed. Let's clear out before anyone ends up in cuffs."

A few people laughed—nervous, performative. One man, shirt torn and lip bleeding, stepped forward like he wanted to test how much patience I had left. I met his eyes, steady. Didn't glare. Didn't flinch. Just waited.

He blinked first.

Behind me, the approaching sirens wailed—sound meeting blue light as the other cruisers turned into the parking lot. The crowd shifted, courage leaking out the edges. They started to move, splintering into groups, tossing curses like breadcrumbs behind them. Within minutes, the noise drained away, leaving only the rustle of gravel and the low hum of the cruisers' engines.

The bouncer appeared in the doorway, wiping his hands on a rag that looked older than the building.

"You got here quick," he said. "Thanks. I thought they were gonna tear the place down."

"You did the right thing shutting it early," I told him.

He nodded, eyes scanning the lot. "Same every warm spell. As soon as the heat hits and the moon's out, people lose their minds."

By the time backup left, the street was empty again. Just crushed beer cans catching light, a single flip-flop abandoned in the gravel. The smell of alcohol and smoke hung as thick as humidity. Somewhere in the distance, frogs croaked like they were stitching the quiet back together.

Top's words came back, as they often did on nights like that—different bar, different year, same damn heat.

"They only see the reflection, not the person behind it. If you start fighting every reflection, you'll forget who you are under it."

Standing there in that empty street, I finally understood. The badge could make you the villain in one story and the savior in the next, and neither version had much to do with the truth. It wasn't just fear that wore you down in this job—it was being seen the wrong way, again and again.

When I got back in the cruiser, the steering wheel was slick with sweat. I turned off the lights and let the engine idle, the night slowly deflating around me. Somewhere out past the marsh, a bottle rocket popped—leftover fireworks from someone's backyard—and for a second it sounded like the echo of a fight that hadn't quite finished.

I wrote the report later at the station.

One paragraph. Clinical.

"Units responded to disturbance at Crosswind Tavern. The crowd dispersed without incident. No injuries. No arrests."

That's all it said.

No mention of the way the crowd had stood there in the headlights, defiant and waiting. No mention of the thought that hit me in that heat— that half the job was learning not to take what people throw at you as truth.

When I hung my uniform at the end of the night, I caught my reflection in my dresser mirror. The badge flashed dull light, smudged from sweat and fingerprints.

For a second, I didn't see a symbol.

I saw a man trying to stand still while the world kept assigning him motion.

It looked tired.

So did I.

Bubbles

It was one of those late-shift Carolina nights when the heat refused to leave and the town felt half-asleep but restless. Saturday was winding down, the worst of the chaos already behind us—no bar fights waiting in the wings, no domestics hanging by a thread. Just a few more hours until shift change and the promise of a shower, a quiet house, and sleep.

I was parked in the corner of a convenience store lot, the kind with flickering lights and a worn-out ice freezer out front. The engine idled low, the A/C trying its best to fight the humidity. My laptop balanced on my knee as I worked through reports—narratives that took messy, loud calls and pressed them into neat, quiet paragraphs.

An older patrol car eased into the lot and rolled up beside me. It was one of our guys. He gave me the kind of nod you reserve for late-shift comrades—part greeting, part we're almost done.

He rolled his window down.

"Let's get a cup."

I didn't need much convincing.

We killed our engines and stepped into the bright hum of the store. Inside smelled like cleaning chemicals and a stale ashtray. We filled foam cups with coffee that looked like it had been on the burner since noon, then drifted back out into the night.

We leaned against our cars, sipping slowly, watching traffic slide past on the four-lane. Headlights moved in steady lines—pickup trucks, tired sedans, and the occasional loud car with too much bass and not enough muffler. We weren't hunting, exactly, but we were hopeful. Sometimes the best DWI cases drive right to you—hit a curb, make the wrong turn, get a little too confident. It happened more often than people thought.

My partner finished his coffee and climbed back into his car, fiddling with his radar unit, angling for a speeder in the last hour of the shift. I stayed outside, the air still hot but softer now, the sky bruised with the last of the night's color.

That's when the limousine pulled in.

Long. White. Gleaming under the streetlights. It glided into the lot like it had taken a wrong turn out of a different zip code. On this side of town you saw work trucks and rusty sedans, not stretch limos.

It rolled to a stop a few spaces away. The engine stayed running. The back window slid down, then the sunroof, then another side window—like a slow reveal.

Laughter spilled out first.

A cluster of women leaned out—hair done, makeup perfect, dresses meant for a night that was supposed to be memorable. In the middle of them, framed by the sunroof, was a girl in a white wedding dress. A tiara sat crooked in her hair. Her grin could've lit half the parking lot.

"Officer!" she called, waving me over. "Can you come here a minute?"

I glanced at my partner. He raised an eyebrow, then went back to his radar, pretending not to listen while listening to everything.

I set my cup on the trunk and walked over.

Up close, there had to be ten of them packed inside—sequins catching the light, bare shoulders, perfume, and laughter spilling into the night. It looked like someone had shaken a bottle of champagne, and all the bubbles had turned into people.

"What can I do for you?" I asked.

The bride leaned forward, elbows on the window frame, veil slipping off her shoulder. There was a mischievous tilt to her smile that should've warned me.

"Our dancer cancelled," she said, like she was reporting a crime. "How much do you charge?"

I blinked.

"For what?"

"To dance for us," she said, as if this were obvious. "You know—take off the cop uniform. Just down to your shorts or whatever. We'll pay you good money. And your partner too."

Somehow, this felt riskier than half the fights I'd broken up.

The limo erupted—cheers, whistles, and clapping. I heard my partner's car door open behind me.

He approached wearing the same serious cop face we used on traffic stops and bar calls.

"Everything okay here?"

They repeated the offer.

His expression cracked. He started laughing before he could stop himself.

I'd been propositioned before—phone numbers scribbled on receipts, comments tossed out during stops—but never like this. Never from a limo full of women in plastic tiaras asking for a striptease instead of directions.

Part of me was stunned.

Part of me—if I'm honest—was curious in that way you get when life veers completely off script.

"Where are y'all headed?" I asked, buying myself a second.

She pointed across the road, still grinning.

"Over there. Little parking lot. You two climb in. Make the night special."

One of them waved a wad of cash like a flag.

I looked back at my partner. He was married. I was married. We were both in full uniform—sidearms on our hips, radios clipped high enough to catch every word. The ice machine rattled behind us, loud and indifferent.

"We appreciate the offer," I said finally, "but we're gonna have to pass. We're on duty."

"And our wives would have a lot to say about it," my partner added.

A chorus of exaggerated groans filled the limo.

"Your loss," the bride said, mock offended. Then she laughed and handed me a napkin with an address scrawled on it. "Just in case you change your mind."

I took it out of reflex. The handwriting was bubbly, with a heart dotting the i. It felt like holding a ticket to a parallel universe I had no business visiting.

"We'll, uh, keep it in evidence," my partner said, deadpan.

They roared again. The limo eased out of the space, girls still waving, jokes flying out the windows. The white dress disappeared back inside like a ghost slipping behind a curtain.

Then they were gone.

I stood there a second longer than necessary, napkin still in my hand.

"I don't think my feet are touching the ground for the rest of the night," I said.

My partner snorted.

"You realize we have to tell dispatch."

He was right. In a small county, dispatch was the heartbeat and the rumor mill rolled into one.

We headed back toward the station. A non-emergency status check lit up the channel, voices chiming in from across the county—deputies, town units, everyone still breathing. We kept our voices straight. When we walked through the door, the dispatchers already knew something was coming.

"You are not gonna believe the call we just turned down," my partner said.

By the time we finished the story, one of them was laughing hard enough to wipe tears from her eyes. The napkin made the rounds like evidence from another dimension. Someone suggested framing it.

For the rest of the night, every time I keyed the mic, at least one voice came back smiling.

We cleared the shift without anything dramatic—no wrecks, no fights, no tragedy. Just quiet streets under a thick summer sky. But that limo stayed with me.

Not because we'd said no.

Because we could have said yes.

Most nights, the stories that stick are heavy—woven with loss and anger and things you don't forget even when you try. But every now and then, the job hands you something absurd and harmless and human.

A hot summer night.

Coffee cooling on a trunk.

A bride in a white dress trying to hire you as a stripper.

We went home laughing.

The napkin stayed folded in my pocket like a private joke between me and the night. For once, the badge wasn't a warning or a weapon—it was a costume in somebody else's story.

Same mirror.

Different reflection.

The light didn't last long. It never does.

The next night, on a new shift, the call came before we'd even found our rhythm.

The Son on the Stairs

The call came across as a family argument, but I knew the family well enough to picture the scene before I even turned onto the street. I'd served beside the father years before in the military and admired him as steady and decent. His wife was kind, the sort of woman who showed up at fundraisers and church suppers with a smile that warmed a room. Their son, though—mid-twenties, no steady job, no relationship—had been drifting. When he drank, he picked fights with the one man who had always stood by him: his father.

His mother met me at the door. Her eyes were red, her voice trembling. She begged me to help without saying it. Behind her, the father slipped past into the yard, head down, the clatter of tools soon following. He lifted the hood on the mower, pretending it needed fixing—his way of saying he couldn't watch anymore, that distance was the only way he could survive being struck by his own son.

At the top of the stairs stood the son, shoulders slouched, one hand pressed awkwardly against his stomach like he was trying to hide something. My gut told me what it might be before my brain caught up. Was it a gun? A knife? Or just another bluff from a young man who couldn't find his footing?

My training kicked in. My voice went sharp, practiced. "Let me see your hands."

He didn't move. His mother turned, saw my gun pointed at her son, and gasped. Her hand flew to her mouth, torn between rushing to him and freezing in terror that I might pull the trigger. Fear and love crashed together in her eyes.

"Show me your hands," I ordered again, louder now, my pulse hammering against the vest. The house felt small and airless. Every creak of the stairs sounded like it could be the one before a trigger pull.

I keyed my mic, "Dispatch, send check-in 10-18."

Sirens rose in the distance as engines roared closer.

Backup arrived, footsteps heavy behind me, radios crackling in the close space. With several of us calling out, pressing from below, the son finally shifted. He descended one step, then another, until he stopped at the landing. His hands came free, empty. No weapon. Just the smell of alcohol clinging to him like a second skin.

I stepped forward and slid the cuffs around his wrists. The click echoed louder than it should have. His mother was crying by then, the sound hollow and ragged.

Relief never came. Only the split in my chest—the officer in me doing his job, the man in me mourning what it would cost them. Charges meant court, lawyers, and bills the family could hardly afford. But letting him go wasn't an option. I'd done what my oath required, but I couldn't shake the question of whether it was what the family truly needed.

This wasn't just another call. It was a reminder that even good families can break, not from one shattering blow but from a slow, steady crack that no one knows how to stop.

As I led him to the cruiser, I wanted to shake him awake, to make him see. Didn't he notice his mother breaking right there in the hallway? Didn't he see how every arrest deepened the fracture in the family that had already given him more grace than he deserved?

That night I carried more than just another domestic report back to the station. I carried the image of a good man hiding in his shed, a mother's heart splintering in front of me, and a son stumbling blind toward a future he couldn't seem to stop destroying.

The cuffs were the easy part. It was everything after—the ghosts, the guilt—that made the badge feel cold in a different way.

*　*　*

After some calls, no one talks. You park two cruisers side by side, engines idling, and just sit there with the radios down low. Someone lights a cigarette even if they quit years ago. You don't discuss what happened—you just share the silence until it stops ringing in your ears. Once, after a particularly bad domestic, one of the older guys turned to me and said, "The trick is not to take it home." I nodded like I understood. But I did take it home. It rode with me, sat in the driveway until the engine cooled, and followed me inside while the house slept. Some things you don't drop at the end of a shift. You just learn how to carry them quieter.

The Last Lesson

That year, the badge began to feel heavier for another reason—one of the voices that had shaped who I was behind it had grown quiet.

Rumors drifted through the station about Top, but none of us wanted to believe he could be sick.

He'd always seemed untouchable—larger than the stories we told about him.

There had been whispers at briefing, quiet pauses on the radio—the kind of talk that travels faster than fact but slower than truth.

"Cancer," someone said. Agent Orange exposure from his time in Vietnam, another added, like naming the poison could make sense of it.

None of us wanted to believe it. Top didn't get sick.

He was built from something the rest of us didn't have—calm, grit, and the kind of patience that looked like armor.

He'd been the standard we measured ourselves against.

The idea that time could reach him felt wrong.

When the word finally came that he was gone, the station went still.

No radio chatter. No nervous jokes. Just the hollow quiet that fills a room when everyone's thinking the same thing.

I sat at my desk long after the others drifted out, staring at his old locker.

Someone had taped a small photo of him there once—grinning in uniform, coffee in one hand, that same smirk that said he saw more than he'd ever tell.

The tape started to yellow, but he still looked alive in it, like he might walk through the door any minute and ask why we were all sitting around.

*　*　*

Later that week, we lined up for the procession.

I was in it—one patrol car among more than one hundred from across the state.

The line stretched for miles, blue lights pulsing in rhythm, a slow river of respect winding through small towns and backroads.

Every overpass was lined with people. Some held flags. Others simply stood with their hands over their hearts.

The hum of the engines and the sight of all those lights moved something deep inside me—the living escorting one of their own home.

At the cemetery, the air was still and bright, the kind of Carolina blue sky that felt too perfect for grief.

The military honor guard stood at attention as the casket was carried forward, each step measured, boots sinking slightly into the soft earth.

The Chief spoke first—short, steady, his voice catching only once.

He said that Top had served with honor, led with grace, and left this world better than he found it.

Then he did something no one expected.

He retired Top's call number. Permanently.

The dispatcher's voice cracked over the radio:

"803, 10-42. Rest easy. We have the watch from here."

Then came the salute.

The honor guard raised their rifles. The command rang out—"Ready, aim, fire."

Three volleys split the air, sharp and final.

The sound settled over the field like a benediction.

For a moment, no one moved. Then the pipes began again, the notes stretching across the open sky.

I found myself remembering the long hours riding in the patrol car, the way he'd stand behind me—arms crossed, voice calm—guiding without ever raising it.

"Slow down. Breathe. Think first."

That was his gospel, and I still carried it.

After the ceremony, I sat in the cruiser with the journal open on my lap.

The pages were smudged from years of calls and silence, but this one stayed clean.

I wrote his name at the top, then below it:

Slow down. Breathe. Think first.

Then, without planning it, I added:

You did. And we learned.

The pipes faded. The crowd thinned.

And for a brief, impossible moment, the world seemed to hold its breath—just long enough for us to do the same.

* * *

Even in death, he held the mirror steady—showing us the best of what the badge could be. Every time I slow down before a call, every breath I take before deciding, he's still there—steady in the mirror.

And maybe that was the quiet truth of it: his voice didn't leave with him.

It just moved—from the passenger seat to somewhere in my chest.

I didn't know it then, but this was the season where his lessons stopped being reminders and started becoming instinct.

We learned early that the uniform wasn't just something we put on—it lived under the skin. Every crease and patch reminded you of what people wanted to see—and what they refused to. Some saw safety. Some saw power. Some saw everything they hated about authority staring back at them.

Over time, that reflection started looking back. You'd catch yourself in a shop window or the side mirror of a cruiser, and you didn't always recognize the eyes staring back. The job changed you in ways slow enough to miss until someone close pointed it out—or stopped pointing it out at all.

That's when you realized the mirror doesn't lie, but it doesn't forgive either.

And when the mirror finally cracks, you turn to the only people who can understand—the ones wearing the same reflection.

Grief wasn't the end of anything—it was the point where everything shifted.

His absence didn't close a chapter; it opened a different one.

From here on, I wasn't just learning the job—I was becoming someone who would one day have to pass the lessons on.

The world kept turning, as it always does after a funeral.

Calls kept coming, and the badge kept asking for more.

The Fire Line

The call came out simple—assist the fire department with traffic control.

I expected to block a road, maybe wave a few cars around. Nothing more.

When I turned the corner, I saw the smoke before the flames. Thick. Heavy. Black.

A pickup truck was on fire in the middle of a rural intersection, its hood blown open, engine compartment fully involved. Heat shimmered off the pavement. Flames climbed twenty feet into the air, licking the branches of a low pine canopy overhead.

A man stood on the roadside, hands shaking, face streaked with soot. Beside him, his wife held their teenage daughter close, her arms wrapped tight around the girl's shoulders. The daughter was crying—silent tears carving clean streaks through the ash on her cheeks.

One of the firefighters told me what happened.

The father was driving home when he smelled something burning. Thought it was a belt, maybe the A/C. He pulled over to check it. When he popped the hood, the engine compartment flashed—old wiring catching fire in a breath. The flames jumped fast, feeding on leaking oil and dry pine needles blown into the frame.

He tried to stop it—grabbed a bottled water jug, a sweatshirt, anything he could find.

But by the time he backed away, the fire had already taken the truck.

"Everything I owned for work is in there," he said, voice hoarse. "My tools. My gear. All of it."

He stared at the burning vehicle like he was watching years of his life melt onto the pavement.

Behind him, firefighters sprayed the engine block, steam rolling off the metal in thick white plumes. The smell of burning rubber and gasoline clung to the air, sharp enough to taste. It stuck to my uniform, my skin, and the night itself.

I stayed until the flames were out and the road reopened.

The quiet that followed didn't feel peaceful. It felt hollow.

You see a lot of types of loss in this job—wrecks, overdoses, violence.

But sometimes it's something smaller that hits hardest.

Not a house.

Not a tragedy.

Just a truck—a man's livelihood, his tools, his pride—gone in minutes.

But that man still had the one thing he couldn't replace.

His wife. His daughter.

The three of them walked away from the fire together.

I thought about that family for a long time.

The way he said it—steady, certain—like he was reminding himself as much as me.

The badge doesn't make you immune to loss.

It just teaches you how to stand beside it.

That's the lesson you don't learn in training—that endurance isn't the absence of feeling, it's what you build after you've felt everything.

The badge asks you to keep showing up, to keep steady hands while the world shakes.

Every officer learns their own version of faith—not in miracles, but in survival.

In the end, that's what keeps you from hardening: not perfection, but persistence.

By the end of that week, I understood the badge doesn't hide you—it mirrors you.

And when the laughter fades, what's left isn't just loss.

It's the reflection you've earned.

Sometimes the reflection looked steady. Other nights, it shook like a hand after a close call. I hadn't yet learned how thin the line was between the shifts that ended in laughter and the ones that left you staring at the ceiling until dawn. The job didn't tell you which kind of night you were walking into—it just gave you a call and let you find out the hard way.

Somewhere in the space between the easy nights and the ones that hollowed you out, the job taught you how to live inside the silence that followed.

Chapter 6—Where Laughter and Loss Meet

Man conquers the world by conquering himself.

—Zeno of Citium

Some shifts rolled in quiet, like the night was giving you a moment to breathe. Others hit without warning, tearing through whatever peace you thought you'd earned. Somewhere between those two extremes lived the job—the stretch of hours where you learned who you were becoming and who you were trying not to be.

The laughter in the squad room, the stories trading hands in parking lots, the quick jokes before roll call—those were the small stitches that kept the seams from splitting. Sometimes it was nothing more than a cup of burnt coffee passed down the line, but it was enough to keep the edge off.

Still, every joke had an aftertaste. Every smile carried the echo of something heavier. One minute you were laughing with the guys; the next you were staring out a windshield after a hard call, wondering how a single night could age you. Grief, guilt, adrenaline, and courage crowded the same narrow space until you couldn't tell where one feeling ended and the next began.

We learned to live there—in the thin space between laughter and loss. Somewhere in that space, brotherhood took root. It wasn't just camaraderie. It was covenant—the unspoken truth that whatever the radio sent your way next, you wouldn't walk into it alone. That promise became its own kind of faith, steadying us when everything else tried to take our footing.

The radio clicked. Someone cleared their throat. A chair scraped against the floor. The night didn't wait for us to finish thinking—it never did.

Two Types of Silence

The first thing you lose in this line of work isn't sleep.

It's the moment silence starts to mean something else.

Before the job, silence is just the absence of sound—something you fill with music, conversation, or the hum of your own thoughts. After the job, silence becomes a place you move through cautiously, like a room you're not sure is empty. You learn to live in that tension—the quiet that steadies you and the quiet that waits to test you.

The first silence comes before the radio crackles, in those seconds when the world feels suspended. Sometimes it finds you at a stoplight at three in the morning, the street empty except for a single moth beating its wings against the windshield. Sometimes it settles in the parking lot after roll call, engines rumbling to life—that breath right before the night begins, when you don't yet know if the shift will leave you untouched or break your heart. It's a thin kind of quiet, stretched tight, like the air itself is waiting to see what you'll do with it.

Dispatch called out another unit number. Someone acknowledged. The world kept moving, even as we stood there listening.

The second silence is nothing like the first.

It fills the car after a call goes bad, when there's nothing left to say—only the rough edge of your own breathing and the weight of what you just saw. It comes after a mother stops screaming. After firefighters drag a hose through what's left of a home. After paramedics close the back doors and drive away with someone you couldn't save. Sometimes there's still the smell of smoke. Sometimes the sound of water dripping off a ruined wall. It's thicker. Heavier. A silence that settles on your chest and doesn't move until you do.

Somewhere between those two, brotherhood is born.

It isn't just shared shifts or dark humor. It's the way someone leans against the cruiser beside you after a hard call, not saying a word because none are needed. It's the look in a partner's eyes when you both walk out of something terrible and know you don't have to explain the part that hurt the most. The quiet hand on your shoulder. The coffee slid across the hood on a night when the weight was finally catching up.

We called it the blue family, but it was closer to covenant—the thin line that held us together when everything else fell apart. An unspoken promise that whatever came, you wouldn't face it alone. That someone would stand beside you at the door you didn't want to knock on. That someone would hear the tension in your voice over the radio and already be on the way.

That promise became its own kind of faith—not loud or spoken, but steady and lived-in. Built shift by shift, call by call, breath by breath. The one thing the night couldn't take.

In the end, it was silence—both kinds—that shaped who we became more than anything the public ever saw. And sooner or later, the night tested which silence you were standing in.

Every shift began the same way—under fluorescent lights, before the radio had a chance to decide.

Roll Call

Nights began in a cramped squad room under humming fluorescent lights— the kind that buzzed just enough to fray your patience. Coffee steamed in chipped mugs stained by years of midnight shifts, the air sharp with starch, sweat, and gun oil. Everyone looked half-dead until the first joke landed. That was the ritual—you laughed before you went back to war.

Roll call wasn't just a meeting. It was a temperature check—not on crime trends, but on each other. You learned more from how a guy slouched in his chair or how tight he laced his boots than from anything on the clipboard. The sergeant ran through BOLOs, warrants, and hot spots, but the real business happened in the side comments, the nods across the room, and the unspoken glances that asked, You good? Are you solid? Are you with us tonight?

The nicknames changed over the years, but the reason for them never did. The names stuck long after the mistakes faded, passed down to new shifts like hand-me-down gear. They weren't fair. They weren't accurate anymore. But fairness wasn't the point. The story mattered more than the truth—because if you could laugh at your worst moment in that room, you could survive the next one on the street.

Nobody was spared, because nobody could afford to be fragile. Teasing was armor—humor wrapped tight over fear, frustration, and the weight none of us had words for. If someone could laugh at himself in that room, you trusted him to hold the line outside. If he couldn't, the night had a way of finding out.

Sometimes the laughter grew so loud it drowned out the hum of the lights. Someone would slam a hand on a locker or reenact a call so badly the rest of us doubled over, tears stinging our eyes. For those few minutes, the world outside—the wrecks, the fights, the domestics waiting to unfold—stopped existing. More than once, I remember thinking this was the last place you ever felt normal before the night decided who you'd be by sunrise.

The sergeant snapped the clipboard shut. Chairs pushed back. Radios chirped to life. Whatever the night had planned, it was already calling us out of the room.

But under the jokes lived something quieter. A shared knowing. Every person in that room had seen something he didn't want to carry alone. That's why we ribbed each other like brothers—because once the clipboard closed and the doors swung open to the night, that laughter was the last piece of light we carried with us. It clung to your uniform the way smoke does after a fire: faint, persistent, and unnoticed until you needed it.

The night didn't care if you were ready. It never does.

But roll call made sure you weren't walking into it alone.

The Chicken Shack

After midnight there was only one place open—a fried-chicken shack by the bypass, grease on the counters, the door slapping shut behind every customer. The coffee was strong enough to strip paint, and the lights flickered like they were tired too. To us, it meant something more than food or caffeine. It was where you went when you needed to breathe again.

When a call rattled someone, you'd hear it quietly:

"Chicken Shack?"

Code for I need to talk.

We'd pile in, shift-worn and bleary-eyed, crowding the corner booth that had heard more confessions than a church pew. Someone always ordered extra chicken biscuits nobody ate. Someone else forgot his wallet. The first laugh was forced. The real one followed.

Some nights we lingered longer than we should have, letting the fryer hum fill the space where words didn't fit. Rookies might sit back and watch, trying to map the unwritten rules—when to joke, when to listen, and when to keep their mouth shut. You could see the moment it clicked: the uniform didn't just come with authority. It came with ghosts, and every ghost had a seat at that table. The Chicken Shack wasn't on any map, but it was where officers learned how to stay intact.

Other nights the conversations were nothing—griping about brass, replaying calls, stretching stories just enough to sound braver or dumber than we really were. And sometimes something heavier slipped out. A look that lingered. A sigh that had nothing to do with work. The Shack didn't fix anything. It just softened the edges enough for us to keep going.

When it closed early or the crowd got too loud, we drifted to the diner down the road—sticky menus, bitter coffee, the same tired waitress who called us "hon." Sometimes she slid an extra slice of pie onto the table and whispered, "On me." Small mercies like that mattered.

Even there, we stayed alert. The uniform drew eyes before you ever spoke. We sat with our backs to the wall, eyes on the door—safe places that never felt entirely safe. It wasn't paranoia; it was a habit, learned the hard way. Each time you put on the badge, you became visible in ways most people never had to consider.

Danger was close. A lingering stare. A window rolling down at a red light. A hand you couldn't quite see. Danger didn't always wait for a call. Sometimes it found you while you were just trying to finish your coffee.

In those booths, though, we were allowed to be human for a while. Stories spilled out—near misses, dumb rookie mistakes, close calls. We laughed until we forgot why. Other times we watched steam rise off our mugs and let the silence settle what we couldn't say.

The diner lights made us look softer. Almost normal. Then the radio cracked, and it was back to the dark.

We left when the sky began to pale, fryer smoke clinging to our uniforms. That little shack, that worn-out diner—they weren't much. But in a job that showed us the worst of humanity, they reminded us we were still part of it—the place where laughter still worked, but loss was never far.

I didn't know then how quickly that stretch could vanish.

How fast routine gives way to something louder.

How the job lets you rest just long enough to forget what it can become.

Then it became something else entirely.

The Storm That Took the Island

The call came while I was home—the kind of call that changes everything before you even hang up.

It was the Chief.

"Storm coming."

"Bring enough clothes, a sleeping bag, and everything you'll need," he said. "You won't be home for at least two weeks—and that's just to pick up clean underwear."

When I stepped outside, the sky was Carolina blue. Not a cloud in sight. Even the birds were quiet, as if they could feel the pressure dropping before we could. It was hard to believe a Category 5 hurricane sat only a few hundred miles offshore, barreling straight toward us.

They staged us inland, at a middle-school gymnasium converted into a Red Cross shelter. Cots lined the front entrance like a barracks. The Chief laid out the plan: four hours on, four off, rotating until we could get back onto the island. I drew the first shift.

By the time I hit the streets, the sky had turned that sickly green you only see before the worst storms. The wind had started to warn of what was coming, breathing hard through the trees as I rolled through neighborhoods with the loud hailer crackling:

"Mandatory evacuation. Leave the island immediately."

Most listened.

A few didn't.

One call came from another officer trying to reason with a business owner who refused to leave. The man stood in his doorway, arms folded, jaw set.

"I'm not leaving," he said. "You can't make me. Everything I've got is here."

The officer nodded, voice calm.

"You're right, sir. We can't make you. But before we go, I'll need your next of kin."

The man blinked.

"Why?"

"So we'll know who to call to identify your body."

Something cracked. He thought about it—really thought about it—but he stayed. We left him a flashlight and a prayer we didn't speak out loud.

Back at the causeway, we closed the high-rise bridge to incoming traffic. I parked near the barricade, the cruiser rocking in the gusts, wipers useless against sheets of rain. Out beyond the dunes, waves rose massive and confused, climbing higher with every surge. We all knew once those dunes failed, the ocean would take the whole island.

When the Chief's voice finally came over the radio, it was the order we'd been waiting for.

"Pull back to the shelter."

The Red Cross was serving rice and beans when I returned. Outside, rain hammered the gym's metal roof in relentless waves. I moved my personal truck beside the building, hoping it might survive the night.

The Chief gathered us under flickering lights. Reports were already stacking up—dunes gone, roads washed out, storm surge flooding from ocean to sound.

"We're not going back until the National Guard arrives," he said.

That night, lying on a thin cot beneath groaning steel beams, I listened to the wind tear at the world outside. The walls shuddered. The roof moaned and lifted a few inches with each breath of the storm. Then the power failed, and the gym went black.

Flashlights cut thin beams across faces turned toward the ceiling. Someone hummed a hymn under his breath. Someone else whispered a joke to break the fear. Even in the dark, we stayed tethered.

I drifted off.

At dawn, I woke to the low growl of diesel engines and the sharp tang of exhaust. The National Guard had arrived in Humvees. Outside, the sky was impossibly blue again—cruel in its calm. The humidity returned in a rush, thick enough to taste.

We loaded into the convoy and rolled back across the bridge. The air still carried salt and diesel, but underneath was something sharper—burnt wood and insulation, broken septic tanks, and the scent of everything that used to be home.

Houses lay scattered in the streets, walls peeled open like matchboxes. Boats sat wedged inside living rooms, bows pressed against shattered televisions and overturned couches. Whole rows of homes were completely gone, ripped from their foundations by waterspouts that had come ashore like monsters.

Then I saw a child's bicycle tangled in seaweed but upright, still red beneath the grime. For a moment, it looked like defiance itself.

The ocean was quiet now—deceptively calm—smoke drifting thin and ghostly from the ruins. Embers had somehow survived the flood. Every so often, a security alarm shrieked into the emptiness, batteries still hanging on, refusing to quit. We stood and listened, letting it echo until it faded.

We stood there a long time, no one speaking, listening to the alarms cry across what was left of the island.

That night, we built a small fire in the middle of the road to keep the mosquitoes at bay. The wood came from broken homes—splintered beams and doorframes dragged clear of the wreckage. The flames stayed controlled, more habit than comfort. We sat close enough to feel the heat, far enough not to need words.

It was the kind of silence shared by people who refused to give up— standing shoulder to shoulder against something bigger than all of us, holding the line after the ocean tried to erase it.

Eventually, the work moved us on. Roads reopened. Power returned in pieces. The island learned how to breathe again, even if it never looked the same.

We went back to calls that didn't make the news—wrecks, arguments, and small violences that still mattered to someone. The badge didn't care what disaster came before it. It just asked you to keep showing up.

And sometimes, showing up looked ordinary again.

Ordinary never meant untouched.

The Crash

We'd stopped to eat at our local pizza joint—the kind of place where the cheese stretched too long, the pizza was greasy, and the neon beer sign buzzed like a tired heartbeat. It wasn't uncommon for a deputy to swing by and grab dinner with us. Over time, a few of them became more than familiar faces—they became family: holiday dinners, bowling nights, and long games of cards on our days off. We knew each other's kids, their favorite jokes, and who burned burgers on the grill every time.

That night, he'd joined us. Just another summer evening—the town alive, the humidity clinging to your uniform like a second skin. We talked about nothing and everything: weekend plans, ball games, and who owed whom for dinner. He laughed that big, easy laugh of his—the kind that made you forget how thin the line really was.

Later that night, the tones hit the radio.

An alert—a pursuit headed toward town. The sheriff's office was chasing a stolen car. The officers' voices came through pitched high, sharp with adrenaline. We listened out of habit and worry, waiting to hear it pass without touching us.

Then silence.

We expected the call to wrap up—maybe a crash, maybe a foot chase. Instead, the tones sounded again. A wreck. A wreck involving a sheriff's car. Too fast around a curve. Lost control.

Then the EMS voice—calm, professional, unbearable. "One fatality. Highway Patrol requesting a supervisor."

We froze. No one spoke. Just minutes ago, he'd been sitting across from us—his half-eaten slice still cooling on the plate. It didn't make sense. It couldn't be him.

Our sergeant left for the scene, five miles down the road. We followed as far as the convenience store at the town limits and waited under the buzzing lights, willing the radio to say something different. When the confirmation finally came, the world tilted—disbelief folding into grief, grief into silence.

We'd just eaten dinner with him.

And now he was gone.

By morning, the flag hung at half-staff, black bands stretched across badges like mourning tape over hearts. At the funeral, the bagpipes cut the air thin. His wife stood in a simple black dress, hands folded, her face set in the quiet shock that hadn't yet found words. Rain beaded on dress uniforms, rolled off polished hats, and darkened the green grass at our feet—a sound so soft it made everything else feel louder. You could see it in every face: that hollow look of someone staring at his own possible ending.

When the service ended, the crowd thinned, and the sound of boots on dry grass was all that remained. We stood beside the cruisers, not ready to leave yet—not ready to face the silence waiting beyond the gates.

Then the radios went still.

We listened—not to our own channel, but to the sheriff's frequency. Their dispatcher's voice came through steady and measured, carrying the weight of what none of us wanted to hear.

"214... 10-42. End of shift."

No one spoke. We stood there under the gray sky, hands resting on hoods, the static fading into the wind. The words hung longer than any eulogy. That was the real goodbye—the one without applause or prayer, just quiet acceptance.

Later, when we finally pulled out of the cemetery, you could still feel it—that final transmission echoing somewhere between grief and gratitude.

We carried him—six of us, shoulder to shoulder, taking him home one last time.

That's what this job teaches you. Not just how to stand together in a fight, but how to stand when one of those shoulders is gone.

That night, we didn't just lose a partner. We lost the laughter that used to hold the darkness back.

And still, the radios stayed on.

Even after the funerals. Even after the last car pulled away. The night kept asking questions. Calls kept coming. Panic kept breaking loose in places that had no idea what we'd just buried.

Grief didn't silence the job—it just changed how we carried it.

The Voices in the Dark

You never see their faces.

You just hear their voices—calm, measured, never quite matching the storm on the other end. They sit in a dim room behind the radios, surrounded by glowing screens and the low hum of fluorescent lights. While we're out here chasing the noise, they're the ones holding the thin line between panic and order. To most people, they're just voices in the dark. To us, they're the tether—the steady thread that keeps us connected to something solid.

They know every one of us by voice.

Before we ever give a call sign, they already know who it is—the gravel of fatigue, the edge of adrenaline, the laugh that slips out when the night runs long. They know who taps the mic twice when they're frustrated, who forgets to release the button when they mutter a curse, and who hums along to the radio between calls. Sometimes it feels like they know us better than we know ourselves.

And they always know when something's about to go wrong.

There's a silence that settles right before it—a breath held too long, a word that catches on the way out. A rookie might miss it. Dispatch never does. They lean forward, already listening for what the rest of the world hasn't heard yet. Then they do what they always do: steady their tone, slow their breathing, and guide us through whatever waits on the other side of the transmission.

I've heard that silence from their side before.

The tones go out clean. Then a pursuit. A foot chase. An officer shouting. And then—nothing. Just dead air. I can still hear one dispatcher calling the same unit again and again, her voice tightening each time until the only sounds left were the ticking clock and the kind of quiet that fractures a room.

When the word finally came back—one fatality—no one spoke. The radio stayed open, waiting for a voice that would never answer. The dispatcher didn't cry. She didn't waver. Her voice stayed steady for the rest of us who were still out there.

That steadiness cost something.

People think dispatchers just answer phones, type notes, and push buttons. They don't see the way they listen. They hear everything—the fear in a rookie's voice, the fatigue in a veteran's, the half-joke someone makes just to stay upright. They're the first to hear a cry for help and sometimes the last to hear it fade. They absorb the panic, the grief, and the screaming—and somehow send us back out calm.

I've seen them at the end of a shift, sitting in that quiet room long after the calls stop. Just them and the low hum of equipment cooling down, voices still caught somewhere in the static. You can see the weight on their faces—the kind that doesn't come with medals or citations. The cost of being the first to hear and the last to forget.

Most people will never see their faces.

That's what it means to be one of the ones who listen.

They don't wear a badge, but they carry all of ours.

They're the calm before the storm, the voice that steadies the moment, and the silence that follows when the line finally clears. Every night we go out, we trust that voice to bring us home.

And every time the radio crackles and we hear, "Unit clear for traffic?"—it feels like a prayer answered.

Because somewhere in that small room, they're still there.

Still listening.

The radio clears. The night exhales. And whatever made it through with you doesn't leave when the sound does.

What We Carry Forward

We used to joke that the uniform came with an invisible weight across your soul. Every laugh, every loss, and every funeral tightened it. But no one ever set it down.

The badge isolates you from the world but binds you to the ones beside you. The public sees authority; we see the faces behind the mic—the people who show up when no one else will. You don't choose that bond; the job forges it. Somewhere between midnight calls and the smell of gun oil, between laughter at roll call and the silence after funerals, it hardens into something that holds.

I used to think the weight was punishment—a reminder of how fragile we were under all that armor. Over time, I learned the truth: the weight is proof. Proof that you still care enough to feel it.

Some nights I'd park in the driveway, kill the engine, and just sit there—collar damp, radio whispering faintly. The engine ticked as it cooled, filling the quiet, reminding me that home had its own kind of noise. Sometimes the weight cut deep—after funerals, when bagpipes faded and boots pressed through wet grass. Other nights, that same burden felt like the only thing keeping you upright.

Brotherhood isn't bravery. It's endurance—the hand that steadies you when you can't steady yourself, the voice on the other end of the radio that says, "I'm right behind you." In time, you realize brotherhood isn't just what saves you—it's what you owe. To every name etched on a wall. To every partner who never made it home. To the part of yourself that still believes something is worth protecting.

Maybe that's why none of us ever really let go. Because even when the shift ends, the weight stays—not as a chain, but as a reminder that love and loss wear the same uniform.

Grief doesn't leave when the bagpipes fade. It lingers—in the empty seat, in the badge you polish, and in the names that still answer in your head long after the radio goes quiet. Some memories stay close because they never finished what they started. Others because you won't let them go.

They live in the pauses—between transmissions, between breaths, between one shift ending and the next beginning. And when the radio crackles again, you take a breath, answer like always, and carry them with you back into the dark.

By the time the worst had passed, I understood that laughter was a kind of defiance. It didn't erase loss—it gave it shape. Some ghosts don't fade with sunrise. They ride home in the passenger seat and wait for quiet.

And it's in that quiet—in the space between what we survived and what we still carry—that the past finally speaks.

The next morning, someone brought bad coffee and worse jokes, and we stood around like nothing had changed. In a way, nothing had. The weight was still there—but so were the people who helped carry it. We talked about the night like we always did, then turned toward whatever came next.

That's how the job worked.

You didn't outrun what followed.

You walked forward together.

Chapter 7—The Ghosts You Carry

The soul becomes dyed with the color of its thoughts.

—Marcus Aurelius

Some losses arrive loudly, announced by sirens and shouted orders, but the real ghosts don't bother with theatrics. They slip in quietly—through a half-remembered scent, a sound you can't place, or the flash of blue light across the inside of your eyelids when you're trying to sleep. You don't invite them, and you don't notice the moment they decide to stay.

Some nights, the ghosts weren't loud at all. They didn't arrive with raised voices or the echo of a call replaying itself. They showed up in smaller ways—a porch light already on when you got home, a dog lifting its head at the sound of the door, and the refrigerator humming like it always had. Ordinary things, still intact.

I'd hang the uniform in the same place, set the keys down, and wash my hands longer than necessary. The water ran clear. The mirror showed the same face it always had. Whatever the night had carried with it, the house didn't ask me to explain it. It just stayed a house.

That was the first time I understood the ghosts weren't there to take more from me—only to remind me that I had made it home. That the job left marks, yes, but it also left me standing. And some nights, that was enough to keep going.

What I didn't understand then was that learning to carry them wasn't surrender. It was a kind of discipline—the same kind the job demanded everywhere else.

One day you're laughing in a squad room, alive in the noise of it; the next, the laughter lands differently, ricocheting off something unseen just out of reach. But even then—even in the shifts where the stillness presses in—you're not facing it alone. Someone always finds their way close, sharing the same silence, the same breath, and the same weight.

Every officer carries a handful of calls that never filed themselves away—calls that didn't end when the paperwork did. They live in the pauses: the breath between transmissions, the hush before dawn, and the moment after you turn the key in the ignition and feel something settle in your chest that wasn't there the month before.

What they don't tell you—what Top tried to teach us before we were ready to hear it—is that carrying the weight isn't failure. It's evidence.

It's a skill you earn slowly, by choosing not to let the weight decide who you become.

Some nights, you can almost pretend you're the same person you were when the badge was still new and the world felt steady. But in the real quiet—the honest quiet—the ghosts step forward again. Not to punish. Not to frighten. But to remind you of what the job cost and what it gave back.

They ride with you on those long drives home, familiar without ever introducing themselves. You carry them—and because of that, you carry each other.

Over time, I learned the difference between being haunted and being shaped. One erodes you. The other teaches you how to keep going without hardening.

The One You Don't File Away

There's a sound that stays with you—the crack of metal folding, the silence that follows. But mostly it's the smell that holds on: scorched asphalt, diesel, and blood baked in the sun. It finds you at the strangest times—filling your gas tank, driving past roadwork, standing too long on a hot highway shoulder. One breath, and the years collapse.

That day was brutal for me—sunlight so harsh it turned the road into a mirage. The kind of heat that shimmered off the blacktop and crawled down your collar. The radio crackled: "Head-on collision, dump truck versus SUV, possible ejection, children on scene." The dispatcher's voice was calm, but the knot in my gut wasn't.

When I arrived, the air was thick: burnt rubber, gasoline, transmission fluid, and the metallic tang that clings to the back of your throat. The SUV lay upside down in the middle of the highway, glass glittering across the asphalt like scattered ice. The dump truck sat in the median, its grille crushed and streaked with dust and debris.

The driver, a young mother, had been ejected through the sunroof. No seatbelt. No pulse. No chance. She lay in the middle of the highway, the sun merciless overhead, heat rising around her in waves.

Her two children stood over their mother, both crying, not the panicked kind, but the kind that empties you out. They were shaking her, tiny hands on her shoulders, whispering through tears, "Mommy, wake up. Mommy, please wake up."

I can still hear it.

I knelt beside her, knowing it was too late, but doing what we always do: checking, hoping, and denying what's right in front of us. The asphalt burned through my pants, but I didn't move.

Other units arrived. One officer led the children away, voice soft but breaking. Another began photographing the scene, the shutter clicking steady as a heartbeat. And then I saw him, the dump-truck driver, sitting on the curb, glassy-eyed, reeking of alcohol. His words came slow and disjointed, like fragments of a dream.

He lived.

She didn't.

Someone brought a white sheet from the ambulance and laid it gently over her. The wind caught its edge, lifting it for a moment before it settled again. A final kindness against the unforgiving heat.

We waited for the medical examiner, for the tow trucks, and for time to start moving again.

I've seen a thousand wrecks since that one, but it's this memory that stays, not the twisted metal or flashing lights, but the sound. Those children's voices, small and desperate, echoing across the asphalt.

You learn to say you're fine. You learn to act like you're fine. But some things don't fade.

The law took him.

They stayed with me.

But staying didn't mean taking over. It meant remembering without losing myself to the remembering.

*   *   *

Weeks later I drove past the same stretch. Someone had tied ribbons to a cross, already frayed and faded from the sun. I pulled over. Some memories demand that much.

Still, the smell lingered. The asphalt baking under a fresh sun, the petroleum stink rising from the pavement itself. Even without the wreck, the air carried an echo of that day. All it took was a moment.

You learn early in this job that not every memory wears a face. Some hide in the senses. Some wait for you in the heat, in the shadows, in the sound of a siren passing in the distance. And some, like this one, hide in the smell.

I used to think Top was talking in riddles whenever he said the mind remembers what the heart won't touch. Back then it sounded like a lesson I wasn't old enough to learn yet. But standing on that stretch of highway, the guardrail ribbons fluttering in the mirror, I finally understood what he meant.

The job teaches you control. Control of fear, control of chaos, and control of yourself. But ghosts don't respect control. They slip past your training, past your armor, past everything you built to keep yourself steady. They remind you that some things aren't meant to be controlled. Only carried.

And this one—this mother on the asphalt, this smell, this sound—it settled somewhere deep, a memory I didn't choose but had to live with. A reminder that calm has a cost. That every lesson in composure comes from a moment when the world gave you no choice but to stand in its wreckage.

*   *   *

Sometimes I wonder about the dump-truck driver—whether he remembers the sound, whether he ever smells diesel on a summer day and freezes. I don't know if the prison sentence changed him. I only know the memory changed me.

The children, now grown, will never know my name. They'll never know who knelt beside their mother. They'll never know who tried to talk them away from the body or who stood with them under that merciless sun. Maybe that's better. Maybe distance is its own kind of mercy.

I carried their voices through every summer that followed. Through every heat wave, every engine, every scorched shoulder of highway. Through every shift when laughter didn't reach, when the radio hum felt thin and hollow, when the Chicken Shack lights seemed too bright.

Some calls fade. Some blur into the edges of the job.

But not all of them break you. Some teach you how to stand still inside the pain without letting it take everything else with it.

But some—the ones that shape you—stay sharp.

Because the ghosts that come quietly don't come to frighten you. They come to remind you. Of what you lost. Of what you carry. Of what the job takes before you realize it's gone.

When the Ghosts First Find You

You don't warn the rookies about the ghosts—not at first. You teach them tactics, safety, and how to survive the shift. You drill them on traffic stops, how to approach a car, and how to keep their gun hand free. But you don't tell them that the danger doesn't end when the call does—that some parts of the job follow you home whether you invite them in or not.

Long before the calls that would stay with me—before the weight ever settled in—Top was steady at my shoulder, shaping the officer I hadn't yet grown into.

Sometimes, when the memories get loud, I think back to where the ghosts first found me—back when I didn't yet understand what they were trying to leave behind.

When my Chief pinned on my badge, I was twenty-one, too young to realize how much I didn't know. My boots still squeaked, and my uniform was creased so sharply it could've cut paper. I thought courage was a skill, something you could master if you tried hard enough. I didn't yet understand how easily it could wear thin.

Top was steady and unreadable—the kind of calm that made chaos look small. He didn't talk much. He didn't have to. His lessons lived in the pauses, in the way he scanned a room, and in the quiet that settled around him before he spoke.

I think back to my first bar fight outside town. Dispatch said, "two males, possibly three." When we pulled up, there were closer to twenty—spilling into the lot, music thumping behind them, glass glittering across the pavement like confetti. Someone shouting, someone bleeding, the kind of heat and noise that felt alive.

Top stepped out and cracked his neck like he'd done this a thousand times.

"Stay close," was all he said.

Inside, the place was a blender—fists flying, alcohol in the air, chairs scraping the floor. Two men were locked up near the pool table, red-faced and wild. A bottle broke somewhere behind me.

Top grabbed one. I moved on to the other—a big, sweaty, mean guy who looked like he'd been saving his bad day for me. When I caught his arm, he spun fast and threw a blind punch that caught my cheek—sharp, hot, teeth rattling. The room tilted.

I hit him with pepper spray. He coughed, grinned through the burn, and growled: "That all you got?"

He swung again.

I sprayed him a second time—a good, full blast—and that finally folded him. He dropped to his knees, clutching his face as the burn hit full force.

For a second, the whole bar froze—coughing, shouting, and half in disbelief.

Top had his guy pinned against the bar. He looked over at me, calm as a Sunday morning, and nodded.

"You good?"

My eyes were leaking so hard I could barely see him. "Yeah," I lied.

Outside, the neon buzzed against the night. My cheek throbbed. My chest still shook with leftover adrenaline. Back at the station, the veterans howled, calling me "Pepper Boy," claiming I'd earned my first war story.

I laughed along—but later, alone in the bathroom, I learned the unspoken rookie lesson: Never touch your face after using pepper spray—and definitely never go to the bathroom before scrubbing your hands.

That mistake teaches itself in one unforgettable second.

As I headed out, Top stopped me near the door.

"Good work," he said quietly. Then, after a beat: "Just remember—it's never over when the call ends."

I didn't understand then. But I do now.

The noise fades. The paperwork gets filed. The drunks sober up. But something stays—the punch, the burn, the truth that a few inches or a few seconds could've changed the whole night.

That's when the ghosts first found me—not in the danger, but in the moment afterward when the room finally went still.

Now, when I look at new recruits—all polish and pride—I want to tell them courage isn't what saves you. It's what shapes you. That every shift leaves something behind, whether you notice it or not.

But I don't.

They wouldn't believe me anyway.

Some lessons can't be taught. Not because they're cruel, but because they require time—and someone steady enough to show you how to survive what you carry.

And with time, you learn the difference between carrying the ghosts and letting them carry you.

And maybe that's the quiet truth: the ghosts don't come to haunt you. They come to mark what you survived—and to teach you that survival isn't loud. It's the quiet decision to keep showing up without letting the past harden you.

The Quiet Apartment

Some ghosts don't come from chaos at all—they arrive in silence.

It came through as a welfare check—routine, like a dozen before it. An elderly man. Lived alone. The neighbors hadn't seen him in days. Mail stacked. Lights off. The kind of call that usually ended with an apology and a sheepish wave through the door.

We knocked. Nothing. Door locked. No movement.

I circled to the back and peered through the window. That's when I saw him—legs in shadow, stretched out in the hallway. Before my brain caught up, something hissed past the glass. I jumped back, clipped a stack of metal trash can lids, and sent them crashing like cymbals in an empty alley.

The cat bolted, tail puffed like it had seen a ghost—which, maybe, it had. My partner laughed so hard he had to turn away.

"Real tactical, hero," he said.

When the property manager arrived, his hands shook as he worked the key. He kept apologizing, like the delay was somehow his fault.

The moment the door opened, the smell hit—thick, sweet, unmistakable. Death announces itself before you even cross the threshold. It settles on your tongue, coats your throat, and lingers in a way no air freshener can touch. It's a smell that bypasses thought and goes straight to memory.

The apartment was dim, curtains drawn tight. I found the switch, and a weak yellow bulb flickered to life, illuminating the stillness that had seeped into everything. The man lay on his back, peaceful in a way that didn't match the air. No struggle. No violence. Just time doing what time does when no one is watching.

We looked for next of kin. Nothing. Only a neat stack of mail sorted by date, a half-eaten sandwich gone solid on the counter, and a row of prescription bottles lined up like soldiers. The television was still on mute, casting blue light across the wall like it had been keeping him company.

One doctor's name kept appearing. I called it.

The doctor's voice was calm, practiced, and sad. Terminal illness. No family. No hospice. Just quiet resignation.

She knew the call was coming. "He was a good man," she said softly.

We waited for EMS. The silence pressed in, thick and unmoving. Even our radios seemed reluctant to break it.

When the EMTs arrived—two young women, both quiet—we helped them lift him. They worked gently, almost reverently, covering him with a clean white sheet before fastening the straps. There's a certain grace in how medical crews handle the dead—a final act of dignity for someone who can no longer feel it.

No sirens. No rush. Just respect.

After they left, the apartment felt smaller, still heavy with what remained. A chair pulled out from the table. Shoes by the door. A calendar still turned to last month. Proof that someone had been here, even if no one had noticed he was gone.

It wasn't a tragedy in the dramatic sense—but the loneliness of it stayed with me. A life lived quietly, ending quieter. No chaos, no crowd—just a room waiting to be noticed.

Outside, the same cat sat on the hood of my cruiser, staring like I was the intruder.

"Yeah," I said, rubbing my neck. "You win."

My partner snorted. "Come on, Soprano. Chicken Shack?"

It was the kind of offer that meant more than food—a reminder that even the quiet ghosts lose some of their weight when someone walks beside you.

The Mirror

Sometimes I caught my reflection in a storefront window—badge glinting, jaw set—and for half a second I looked like everyone's idea of a cop: unshakable, composed. Then the light shifted, and the cracks showed. Exhaustion under the eyes. A stare that didn't quite focus. The face I used to fear becoming.

At roll call, the mirror was worse. Same uniform, same badge, but someone different behind it. I used to joke with rookies that you know you've "made it" when your smile stops reaching your eyes. It stopped being funny the morning I tried to smile and nothing moved.

That was when I started remembering something Top told me years earlier.

It was one of those long nights when the town seemed to hold its breath—quiet enough to hear the cruiser's tires whisper over seams in the asphalt. Top reached over and tapped my duty belt.

"Cops are like Batman," he said. "Tool belt around the waist. Difference is, ours can save or scar."

He thumbed through the gear like a rosary—OC spray, cuffs, Taser, baton, gun, magazines, and radio. "Designed for options," he said. "Lethal and non-lethal. But don't kid yourself. Even with hours of hands-on training, this job can hurt people—on purpose and by accident. That's the truth you carry."

He took a long drag from his cigarette, eyes narrowing through the smoke.

"We train to make decisions that change lives in fractions of a second. One wrong read, one wrong move, and everything shifts. Then come the armchair quarterbacks… like they'd have done better. But they weren't there. They didn't smell the gunpowder or see the hands twitch. They didn't feel the heartbeat under the badge."

Top turned back to the windshield, eyes scanning doorways, hands, and rooftops—always rooftops.

"Your first duty," he said, "is to choose right. Your second is to live with what happens when right still leaves a bruise."

He didn't say another word after that. He didn't need to.

Years later, I finally understood what he meant.

I felt the weight of the belt differently—not just the drag on my hips, but the gravity of every choice it carried. On nights I came home, I laid each piece on the dresser like bones from a story: the Taser that worked, the spray that didn't, the cuffs that clicked one notch too tight, and the spare mag I was grateful not to need.

My wife would ask how the shift went.

"Quiet," I'd say, because how do you explain a night where nothing happened except the part inside you that got older?

The ghosts showed up quietly, patient as rust. Not the dramatic kind—no chains, no knocking. Just faces: a boy who ran and shouldn't have, a woman who needed a softer voice, and a man who heard only my volume and not my command.

Some deserved the steel. Some deserved mercy. Some got the wrong one first.

Sometimes, in the cruiser's side window, I catch one riding shotgun—a shape, a shadow, a face I can't quite name. They never speak. They don't need to. They live in the space between what I meant and what happened.

When I pass a dark window now, I try to hold my own gaze—not to see if I look fearless, but to see if I look honest. The badge didn't make me bulletproof. The belt didn't make me someone else.

They just gave my fear and my choices a place to live—and a weight I'm still learning to carry right.

Sometimes I wonder what Top would say if he saw me now. Maybe he'd light a cigarette, nod toward the belt, and tell me the same thing he told me years ago:

Live with the bruise.

The Lonely Chair

When the town finally went quiet—no calls, no chatter, just the wind—I'd step into the business district and start shaking doors.

It wasn't exhaustion that pushed me out there; it was habit, rhythm, a way to settle the night so it didn't settle me. The storefront glass caught my flashlight in quicksilver flashes as I walked past. The wind rolled in from the water, cool and steady, carrying the clean smell of marshland.

On the docks, ropes tapped masts in a slow, measured beat.

Once, a heron glided across the Sound, its wings slicing through the moon's reflection. For a second, it looked like a promise—grace skimming over dark water, heading somewhere certain.

After rounds, I'd head toward the waterfront and sit in that lonely chair—the one facing the harbor. The paint was chipped and the metal cold, but it didn't feel lonely at all. From there, the whole world opened up. The moon climbed higher, laying a pale path across the channel like an invitation to the next day.

That chair became a small sanctuary, not because it escaped the job, but because it reminded me there was more beyond it.

I'd let my thoughts drift to the things that steadied me: my family asleep a few miles inland, the partners who'd rib me at roll call in a few hours, the laughter waiting in the squad room, and the plans I'd made for the next off-day—barbecue, fishing, maybe a ball game.

The job carried weight, sure, but that chair reminded me there was more waiting than ghosts.

Sometimes a fishing trawler hummed past, heading out early, deck lights glowing like warm lanterns. Other nights the harbor lay perfectly still. Even the seagulls perched quietly on the pilings, like sentries standing watch.

Now and then I caught my reflection faintly in a shop window—badge dimmed, shoulders relaxed, eyes not haunted but thoughtful. Not the hardened cop strangers imagined, just a man taking stock of the night and the life beyond it.

The chair didn't judge. It grounded me.

When the breeze shifted, it carried signs of the world waking—rigging clattering, a truck downshifting on the bridge, waves brushing the seawall in their patient rhythm. Dawn always came on slow, brushing color back into the water like someone easing up a dimmer switch.

The town would wake soon, and patrol would start again—morning walkers to greet, alarms to check, and partners to laugh with. But in that sliver of night, it was just me and the water and the sense that tomorrow held more good than bad.

Those hours weren't an escape so much as a reminder: the night gives way to morning, family waits at home, brotherhood waits at the station, and no matter how heavy a shift gets, you don't walk into the next one alone.

Just a man in a crooked chair, watching the harbor settle under the moon, feeling tomorrow lean a little closer.

I didn't go to that chair to escape the ghosts—I went there to see past them.

Those nights still rode along, but from that chair they felt smaller than the life waiting on the other side of the shift.

I was lucky. I found something that helped me see past the ghosts without feeding them.

Not everyone does.

When the job keeps pressing and the quiet won't come, officers learn to reach for whatever softens the edge fastest. And for a lot of good cops—ones who still showed up, still laughed, still wore the badge right—that thing waited at the bottom of a glass.

The Bottle and the Badge

Not everyone finds a place to set the weight down.

It starts small.

One drink to unwind.

One to help you sleep.

Then another.

Then one more because you're afraid of what might happen when you close your eyes.

That night, I stared at the bottle too long. For a moment, the thought came—how easy it would be to make the noise fade into the background.

What nobody tells you is how easy it is to hide the slide. We joke at roll call, we sit at the Chicken Shack, and we ask, "Are you good?" a hundred times a month—but it's a question we rarely answer honestly. You learn early how to look fine even when you're not. The uniform teaches you how to carry weight without showing the strain.

There was a stretch of months I can't account for clearly—nights blurred together by the smell of whiskey and leather. I told myself it helped me sleep. Really, it helped me forget. And because I kept showing up, shining my boots, and filing my reports, no one saw the unraveling.

None of us are trained to spot a man falling apart when he's still standing tall.

I wasn't the first. I wouldn't be the last.

Some claw their way back—faith, therapy, family, a stubborn will that refuses to quit. Some don't. The uniform hides the difference until it doesn't.

When the news reports another officer lost to suicide, we all go quiet. We know it's never one thing. It's a thousand small nights whispering in the dark and one night when someone finally listens.

But there's another truth we don't say enough: sometimes a cop gets saved long before he breaks—not because he asks for help, but because someone reaches out and refuses to accept the mask.

For me, it happened on an ordinary night—no dramatic moment, no flashing lights. Just a quiet shift change, the station humming low, and a sergeant asking, "You good?" in a way that didn't feel like a box-check.

I lied, like we all do. But the question stayed with me longer than the whiskey ever did.

Weeks later, I poured a drink, caught my reflection in the dark window, and froze. I didn't look tired—I looked hollow, like the men I'd buried. Their faces lined up behind mine in the glass, reminders of how easily the job can swallow you whole.

That was enough.

I dumped the glass, called a buddy, and told him to meet me at the diner. He didn't ask why. He just said, "Give me ten."

We didn't talk about the why. We didn't have to. We sat there in that booth, two cups of bad coffee cooling between us, both alive.

Sometimes that's the win.

At one point he nudged his mug toward mine and said, "Tomorrow's a clean slate."

Simple. Unpolished. Real.

And for the first time in a long while, I believed it.

My brother didn't need details. He just needed to show up—and he did. Sometimes all it takes to save a man is another heartbeat on the other end of the line. Someone who knows your ghosts, your silences, your routines, and stays. That was the moment I understood the difference between endurance and healing—and that brotherhood, when it works, makes room for both.

I walked out of that diner lighter than I walked in. Not cured. Not fixed. Just steady enough for the next shift.

And sometimes, that's enough.

Because the truth is, the badge can weigh heavy.

But it's the hands that reach for you—not the bottle—that keep you upright when the night gets too loud.

I used to think strength meant handling it alone. The job taught me otherwise.

And the real test came later—not on the street, but in the quiet moments after the shift ended.

The Driveway

Every night ended the same—headlights sweeping across my porch, the engine ticking into silence. I'd sit there for a few seconds, hands still on the wheel, the smell of the shift clinging to the air. Ten seconds before stepping out.

Ten seconds to pretend I could leave it all in the car.

The truth was, some nights I did. Some nights I didn't. And that was okay.

It happened every night, not one night—a ritual as familiar as locking my cruiser or signing out for the shift. Before I killed the engine, I'd let the radio play a little longer—my music, not dispatch. Something steady. Something that reminded me there was a world outside patrol beats and problem-solving. The dashboard glow washed over the cabin, soft and blue, a quiet I'd earned one mile at a time.

For a few minutes, it was just me, cooling metal, and music humming low like a heartbeat finding its rhythm again.

That vibration stayed in my arms after the motor settled—a reminder of motion, of corners turned, streets cleared, and problems handled. Some nights that rhythm felt like weight. Other nights it felt like purpose.

Either way, it told me I was still moving, still standing, still part of something bigger than the shift I'd left behind.

I'd think about the night—the people, the noise, the strange moments, the good ones—and repeat the old rule: don't bring it inside. Let the house stay on untouched ground. Some nights that worked. Other nights, the stories followed me to the door like they wanted one last word.

But home had its own way of leveling things.

On the good nights, I'd step inside and feel the comfort of small sounds—the creak of the floor, the hum of the refrigerator, my son asleep down the hall with one arm thrown above his head, breathing slow and sure, like the world hadn't asked anything of him yet. I'd stand there longer than I needed to, watching his chest rise and fall, letting that steady rhythm remind me where I was supposed to be.

In the kitchen, there was always proof my wife had been up before dawn—breakfast set out, orange juice in the refrigerator, things placed gently, not hurried. She knew I'd go straight to bed. She did it anyway. Not to be thanked. Just to make sure something solid waited for me when I came home.

On the harder nights, I'd pause in the doorway, still half-cop, half-human, trying to switch gears. My wife always knew which version of me walked in. Sometimes she didn't say anything at all. She just waited—patient in that way only people who truly know you can be—until the words came on their own.

She didn't pull me apart to fix me. She didn't tell me how to feel. She stayed close and steady, letting the weight loosen a little at a time. And between her quiet care and my son sleeping down the hall, I could feel myself come back to the surface—not all at once, not dramatically, just enough to breathe.

Every now and then she'd reach across the table and touch my hand—a small thing, but enough to remind me I was more than the uniform, more than the shift, more than whatever I thought I should've done differently. And when I finally ran out of words, she'd smile that calm, stubborn smile and say, "You did what you could. You're my hero."

It didn't erase anything. It didn't need to.

It brought me back. It reminded me why I kept showing up, why the job still mattered, and why the hard nights never had the final say.

Eventually, I'd close the cruiser door, walk toward the porch light, and feel the weight settle into something steadier—not gone, just shared. The ghosts didn't vanish, but they didn't walk ahead of me anymore.

They fell in step behind me, quiet and manageable, exactly where they belonged.

I used to think ghosts haunted places. Later I realized they lived in the people who cared enough to stay. The trick wasn't forgetting—it was learning who helped you balance it, who waited at the kitchen table, and who made the night feel a little less heavy.

And here's the truth I didn't see back then: by the time I reached that porch light, the bad parts of the shift were already fading—not erased, just outnumbered. Outnumbered by the laughter waiting at the station. Outnumbered by the absurd calls that made no sense then and even less sense now.

Outnumbered by the stories we'd tell later, cracking up over things that should've broken us but didn't.

Because even the darkest nights carried a lighter side—and after the driveway, after the quiet, after the weight settled, that was usually what came next.

Tomorrow always brought its share of chaos and comedy.

And when the comedy hit first, it reminded us we were still alive.

Chapter 8—Finding Light in the Chaos

Life is very short and anxious for those who forget the past,
neglect the present, and fear the future.

—Seneca

For every nightmare, the job eventually hands you something absurd enough to make you laugh. Not because the work is easy—but because laughter is how you survive it. Humor pulled us back into the present, back into breath.

And the strange thing is, the laughter always seems to arrive exactly when you need it most. You can be standing over a wreck that took years off your life or walking out of a call that left your shoulders knotted tight when dispatch chimes in with something ridiculous. You look at your partner. You look at the radio. And something in you finally exhales.

A cracked joke in the cruiser could clear a whole shift's worth of weight in ten seconds. A bizarre arrest could turn into station folklore before the ink on the report dried. Weeks later, rolling back through the same beat, you'd catch yourself smiling—standing right where you once tried to reason with a guy wearing nothing but cowboy boots and a cape. That kind of laughter hits different after midnight—sharp enough to cut through whatever the shift tried to pin on your shoulders.

Most shifts lived somewhere in the middle—between the moments that tightened your chest and the chaos that made you snort-laugh in a parking lot. Somewhere between the story you'd never tell your family and the one your partners would never let you forget.

That's where this chapter lives—

in the moments that reminded us the job was heavy,

but the brotherhood made it lighter.

* * *

In our world, humor wasn't a break from the job—it was part of how we carried it.

It showed up uninvited: a drunk insisting he was "perfectly sober" while dancing in a parking lot; a suspect taking off running only to launch himself straight into a marsh; a hot mic broadcasting more than it ever should. And every so often, it was me—standing in the middle of a scene trying to look composed while holding a pair of cowboy boots some cop insisted were "evidence."

You could go from heartbreak to hilarity in minutes.

If you couldn't hold both, the job would roll right over you.

Even on the hardest nights, the darkness never got the final say.

That balance—between pressure and release—was part of the craft. You learned when to clamp down and when to let the moment breathe. Miss either one, and the job would find a way to correct you.

The Naked Negotiator

It was just after 10:00 on a cloudless Carolina morning, the kind of day that feels too blue and too easy for anything strange to happen. Dispatch sent me to check on a "broken-down vehicle" blocking traffic at a local intersection.

When I arrived, I had to pause. The car sat sideways in the middle of the intersection, angled like it had just lost an argument with geometry. I stayed in the cruiser for a moment, trying to imagine how anyone could have managed to break down in that position on purpose.

I called in the plate, stepped out, and walked up to the driver's side. Behind the wheel sat a woman in her mid-thirties, hair wild, eyes glassy, and wearing the kind of confidence only bottom-shelf liquor can give.

"Ma'am," I said, "can you step out of the vehicle?"

She opened the door, and a half-empty bottle of something amber rolled out and shattered on the asphalt. The smell hit like a distillery in

August. She tried to explain something about car trouble but lost track of the sentence halfway through.

There was no point in sobriety tests. She was well past walking a straight line, let alone touching her nose. I told her to sit back in the car and hand me the keys. She dropped them twice before I finally got them.

Back in my cruiser, I ran her license and called for a highway patrol trooper to handle the breath test—standard procedure. The dispatcher came back with a thirty-minute ETA. Perfect.

When I returned to the car to make the arrest, I stopped cold.

She was completely naked.

Just sitting there, hands folded in her lap, as if this was the next logical step in roadside negotiations.

I blinked.

For half a second, my brain tried to reboot itself, the way it does when a situation is so absurd that professionalism and disbelief collide at the same intersection.

"Ma'am, why did you take your clothes off?"

She smiled—that slow, unfocused grin of someone who still believes charm is a valid legal defense. "I thought maybe we could work something out."

I'd seen a lot on this job, but that one caught me flat-footed. I wasn't laughing. Not yet.

That was my cue. I took a step back, keyed my mic, and called for a female officer, reminding myself to breathe through the absurdity.

When backup arrived, she took one look at the scene and started laughing. "You've got to be kidding me," she said. "You always find the good ones."

I didn't argue. Her laughter hit first, and only then did the tension in my shoulders finally let go—the kind of release that reminds you how much you'd been holding in.

The female officer handled it from there. She made the woman get dressed and transported her to the station for processing. Turns out our naked negotiator was a regular—a habitual drunk most of the shift already knew by name.

Later, when she walked her into booking, the trooper looked up, smirking. "She's yours this time?"

I nodded. "Lucky me."

*　*　*

By the end of the shift, the story had already made the rounds through the county. Word travels fast when absurdity outruns the radio. By roll call the next morning, the jokes were waiting: "Heard you made a new friend last night," and "You sure you're not working vice now?"

By roll call, the story wasn't hers anymore—it belonged to the whole shift.

Stop-Sticks

It was one of those rare Saturday nights—cool air, clear sky, the kind of calm that feels like a dare. The county lay still, too still, like it was holding its breath and waiting for someone stupid enough to ruin the peace.

A few of us had just piled into a convenience store for bad coffee and stale doughnuts when the tones snapped through the radios.

"Unit in pursuit."

We all froze. Then a second alert. And the kicker:

"The sheriff is primary."

Every head lifted. Every eyebrow went up.

When the sheriff himself is behind the wheel, something big is brewing—or about to get real stupid in a hurry.

The radio exploded with life. Sirens in the background, overlapping transmissions, and deputies shouting out mile markers and cross streets like a county-wide warning siren. Someone called out that the chase was cutting straight toward us.

We moved.

Two minutes later, we were staged on the shoulder of the highway, lights flashing, stop sticks unrolled, waiting in the thin slice of darkness between two state highways.

Then—headlights.

They appeared over the rise fast, too fast, climbing the hill like a white-hot comet. The suspect's car tore past our position in a wind blast that made our cruisers rock on their shocks. One rookie swore it peeled the decals off his driver's side door.

The sheriff was right behind him, engine roaring, pushing the car to its absolute edge—a sound driven less by the engine than by the man behind the wheel.

We threw the sticks.

The suspect saw them at the last possible heartbeat. The car jerked sideways, tires screaming as he threaded the needle and missed clean by inches, driving through the trap like he'd rehearsed it.

But we had backup.

Two more units were staged half a mile ahead, tucked near a rural turnoff, waiting to funnel him into a hard right. A simple plan. Clean. Coordinated. As foolproof as the county could manage.

And it worked—almost.

The suspect hit the bend just like we expected. He caught sight of the next set of stop sticks a split second too late, yanked the wheel, and missed them by a hair.

The sheriff didn't.

He hit them dead center, the full weight of the cruiser slamming onto the spikes. No dramatic blowout, no Hollywood sparks—just that soft, unmistakable whup-whup-whup as the hollow steel cores did their job, punching a slow death into all four tires.

The radio hissed with open mics, nobody quite ready to say what we'd just watched.

His cruiser sagged almost immediately, dipping and wobbling toward the shoulder of the road.

Silence. Then the radio clicked.

"Dispatch," the sheriff said, voice steady but absolutely finished. "Send me a wrecker. I, uh… lost the suspect."

We rolled up behind the sheriff a few minutes later.

The sheriff stood next to his dying cruiser, blue lights washing over him in flickering waves. He watched all four tires slouch into the dirt like they were giving up the ghost. He shook his head once, like he couldn't believe the physics himself.

"I should've seen that coming," he said. "That one's on me."

Before any of us could open our mouths, the sergeant's voice chimed in, cheerful as a church greeter:

"Suspect wrecked out up ahead. He's in custody."

The sheriff exhaled—half defeat, half laugh.

"Well," he said, deadpan, "at least somebody caught him."

We held in the laughter until later—at least until he was out of earshot—but the story didn't stay quiet. Stories like that never do.

Five Minutes Out

It was a summer-blue-skies kind of day. I was parked on the shoulder, hand-held radar gun resting on the window frame, half-listening to the radio chatter.

Then the blip came.

Eighty miles per hour. In a forty-five.

I looked up just in time to see a cherry-red Camaro—late model, beautifully restored—flying down the hill like it was auditioning for a movie. I flipped on my blue lights, and before I even merged out, the driver was already pulling over. That was unusual. The ones doing eighty usually need a hint or two.

I stopped behind him, stepped out, and walked up along the driver's side. The car was gleaming in the sun—polished chrome, spotless paint. Inside, a young man sat, knuckles gripping the wheel, license and registration already in hand.

He looked like every nervous driver I'd ever stopped—until he spoke.

"Officer, my wife's having a baby!"

I blinked. "She's at the hospital?"

A dozen possibilities shot through my mind—panic, urgency, and that old helplessness from years earlier, rushing toward a delivery room I couldn't control.

Without pause, he said, "No, sir—she's in the back seat!"

That's when I looked.

There she was—a young woman, maybe in her mid-twenties, legs up on the seat, face red, sweating, breathing hard. It didn't take a medical degree to see she was about five minutes from making me earn a new merit badge.

Her breathing came in sharp, uneven bursts, each one louder than the engine, like she was trying to outrun the moment from the back seat.

I froze for half a second. The mental Rolodex of training kicked in.

Airway, breathing, circulation—no, that's not it. Delivery? Towels? Gloves? Jesus!

I grabbed my radio and called for EMS, trying to sound calm. "Dispatch, I've got a female in active labor—send medical, 10-18."

The husband's eyes were wide, hands shaking. "She said her water broke about ten minutes ago!"

"Of course it did," I thought.

I told him to stay calm—which, in retrospect, is one of those things people say only when they have no idea what else to do.

EMS arrived fast—faster than I've ever seen an ambulance show up, probably because my voice cracked halfway through the radio call. They took over with professional calm, loading her up and assuring the husband she was close but stable.

I stood back by my cruiser, heart still pounding, trying to remember if I'd left the radar gun on.

The young man came over, looking dazed and grateful, and still holding his license like it was proof he hadn't meant to speed. "Am I getting a ticket, sir?"

I shook my head. "Not today."

He smiled, still half in shock, then followed the ambulance as they pulled away—blue sky, sunlight glinting off the Camaro, a good ending to what could've been chaos.

When I got back to the station, I wrote the report under "assist to EMS." A few hours later, a nurse from the hospital called dispatch to pass along a message: it was a boy.

I never met them again. But sometimes, when I'd drive that stretch of road, I'd think of that morning—of how fast life can change in one radar beep.

And of how close I came to adding "delivery room assistant" to my résumé.

I decided radar duty was safer.

* * *

What stayed with me wasn't the panic or the rush—it was how fast the job could pivot from enforcement to mercy. One moment you're clocking speed, the next you're standing between a young family and a moment that will define their lives forever. That morning reminded me that the badge isn't just about stopping danger—it's about meeting people where their world is breaking open and staying steady long enough to help them through it.

Sometimes that means running toward chaos.

Sometimes it means slowing everything down.

Sometimes the job isn't about stopping danger—it's about standing steady when life decides not to wait.

The Bed & Breakfast Heist

It was around 16:00 when dispatch sent me to a robbery call at a local bed and breakfast. That alone made it strange. We handled plenty of calls in motels, bars, and apartment complexes—but never in a Victorian home with flower boxes and a wraparound porch.

The house sat on a one-way street lined with oak trees, the kind of road that still looked like the 1800s refused to leave. When I pulled up, a man came running from the porch, shirt untucked, hair wild, and panic written all over him. My backup parked behind me and stepped out as I approached.

"What's going on?" I asked.

The man took a breath. "I was at the bar having a few drinks, playing pool. Two women came up to me. Said if I bought a bottle of liquor, they'd come back here with me and party. So I did. We got here, started drinking, and... well, things started happening."

He looked embarrassed now, eyes darting toward the ground. "I put my pants on the chair—my wallet was in them. Just got paid—the whole month's salary in cash. Next thing I know, the pants are on the floor, and my money's gone. I confronted them, but they tried to leave."

A flicker of shame crossed his face—the kind that makes you remember how many ways people can get in over their heads.

"Where are they now?" I asked.

"In the room," he said.

We left him outside and walked in.

A stale mix of perfume and cheap liquor hit as soon as we opened the door. I recognized one of them. Local prostitute. The one with the butcher knife.

"Perfect," I thought.

The two women stood by the bed, acting like they'd just been invited to a tea party. I did a quick scan of the room—a liquor bottle, clothes in a heap, nothing subtle about it.

I called for a female officer to assist with the search. When she arrived, I briefed her. "One of them has the cash, but it's not visible. Probably hidden somewhere that's going to require a trip to the ER and a search warrant."

She nodded, then turned to the women. "Here's how this works. You can go into the bathroom, handle it yourselves, and come back out with the money—or we go to the hospital and a doctor finds it for us."

The two exchanged looks. A brief moment passed. Then one of them sighed, turned, and went into the bathroom.

A minute later, the door opened. She stepped out and placed a tight roll of cash on the counter. It landed with a faint slap—soft, final. Her face was blank. No apology, no attitude, just resignation.

The victim stepped forward, picked up the roll, and started counting. His fingers trembled slightly, the sound of bills sliding together filling the silence. When he finished, he looked up.

"It's all there," he said quietly, relief and humiliation wrestling for space in his voice.

I nodded once, logged the serial numbers, and gave him the cash. Both women were arrested for larceny.

Back at the station, the story spread before the paperwork was even done. By the time I walked into roll call the next morning, it had already been retold a dozen times—each version a little funnier than the last. Someone had even left a note on the bulletin board that read:

"When in doubt, check the B & B."

There's no manual for human embarrassment—only the steady way you help someone stand back up.

The Peeping Tom

And every now and then, the job reminds you that not all strange calls are funny—some are quiet, dark, and best handled with your guard fully up.

It was early, around 22:00, one of those nights as black as coffee left too long on the burner. Dispatch called out a "suspicious person" at the Willow Creek Apartments—third peeping-tom call this month.

One of my backup officers was out sick. The other was stuck at the magistrate's office with a drunk who'd decided to argue philosophy through the booking window. That meant no backup for at least twenty minutes.

I parked on the opposite side of the complex, lights out, and stepped into the night. The air had that heavy pressure that only comes before trouble. Flashlight in hand, I made my way between the buildings, moving as quietly as someone wearing a vest and thirty pounds of gear can.

Like a leopard—or at least that's what I told myself—I crept along the edge of the last building, eyes scanning the shadows. Then I saw him.

Face pressed to a ground-floor window. Completely focused.

I inched closer. For a split second, our eyes met—the universal cop-to-suspect moment of "Oh, hell."

Then he bolted.

This guy didn't run like a normal person. He ran like he had trained for it. Olympic-sprinter fast. I took off after him, boots hitting pavement and my flashlight bouncing. But within seconds, he cut through the tree line and vanished into the woods. He knew the complex better than I did.

I stopped, breathing hard, listening. Nothing. No backup. Just me and my heart pounding in the dark.

I circled back to the apartment window he'd been staring into. The blinds were still open. Inside, a young woman sat on the couch in pajama pants and a T-shirt, watching TV, completely oblivious she'd just had an audience.

I recognized her. She worked the late shift at the Chicken Shack—eyes always carrying the weight of too many customers and not enough breaks.

I went to the front door and knocked. She answered, surprised to see a uniform on her porch. I explained what had happened—the man at her window, the chase, and how lucky she'd been that he ran instead of stayed.

Her eyes went wide. "Oh my God. Right here?"

"Right here," I said. "Might be a good idea to keep your blinds closed at night. And don't answer the door unless you know who's there."

She nodded quickly. "Yes, sir."

As I talked, I noticed other apartment doors cracked open. Faces peeking out. Half the complex was trying to eavesdrop. Nothing travels faster in a small town than curiosity.

When I walked back to my cruiser, the whole place had that uneasy shiver in the air again—the kind that settles in when people realize how thin their walls really are. Normally, we'd flood the area with cruisers and dogs, but not that night. It was just me.

So I parked in the lot and stayed there for a while. Partly because I'd been duped by a track star with bad intentions.

Mostly because I couldn't shake the thought of that soft-spoken woman on the couch, watching TV, blinds open to the world.

By morning, the adrenaline is gone—but the image stayed. Some calls don't linger because they were loud or dramatic, but because they showed you how close the dark can stand without making a sound.

The Sleepwalker

We had just started our four on, the long stretch of nights that always came with winter's edge. The holidays were close, and the town had that uneasy quiet that settles in before December—the kind that makes every empty street feel like it's holding its breath.

For most officers, the shift from day to night and back again was brutal. Your body never caught up. One week you were eating breakfast at sunrise; the next, you were having dinner at midnight. Some tried to beat it with workouts before going home, burning off the adrenaline until exhaustion forced sleep. Others leaned on alcohol or prescription sleep aids.

Nobody had found the perfect answer. Night shift wore on you in ways no uniform could hide.

It was around 03:00 when the call came in. The dispatcher's voice sounded off, uncertain.

Tones. "Units respond," she said. "Report of a domestic disturbance at an officer's residence. Possible shots fired."

The silence that followed said everything.

The sergeant keyed up. "Repeat. Did you say an officer's house?"

"Affirmative," she replied. "Officer stated he came home and found his wife in bed with another man. An altercation ensued. Subject reports he shot the male."

Every cruiser in the town went 10-18—lights and sirens.

We all knew the name. A steady officer. Ten years in, he rarely raised his voice and never drew unnecessary attention. The kind of guy you called dependable.

We flew down the highway, engines howling against the cold. Dispatch tried to raise the caller again, but there was no response. The only thing worse than a domestic is a domestic involving one of your own. Emotion, rage, and access to weapons—nothing good ever came from that mix.

When we entered the neighborhood, everything was still. Too still. No lights, no movement, no neighbors outside. Just the faint hum of Christmas lights strung along porches, flickering like they were holding on to warmth.

We blacked out a block away, coasted in, and parked along the curb. The sergeant led us up the walkway, flashlights off. You could hear the gravel under our boots, the shallow sound of breathing, and the soft click of safeties disengaging.

We knocked. No answer.

Knocked again, harder.

Still nothing.

The sergeant called for SWAT to stage nearby in case entry was needed. The air felt electric, that edge-of-the-storm tension that tightens every heartbeat before a breach.

Then, suddenly, the porch light came on. A second later, the house glowed from inside. The living room. The hallway. The kitchen. Each light blinked awake in a slow, sleepy rhythm.

The front door opened.

Standing there in a robe, blinking against the light, was the officer's wife. Her hair was tousled, her face still soft with sleep.

"What's going on, guys?" she asked.

The sergeant lowered his weapon slightly. "Ma'am, we got a call about a domestic disturbance here. Where's your husband?"

She frowned, still half-asleep. "He's in bed. Sleeping."

The sergeant glanced at me, eyes narrowing. "Can we see him?"

She stepped aside. We entered cautiously, clearing each room by instinct. The house smelled like laundry detergent. Nothing out of place. No overturned furniture, no blood, no signs of struggle.

We found the officer asleep in bed, breathing slowly and steadily. The television glowed on mute, washing the room in blue. His service weapon sat holstered on the nightstand.

The sergeant leaned down and touched his shoulder. "Hey, wake up."

Startled, he began to stir, eyes unfocused. "What's going on?"

"You called in a shooting," the sergeant said. "Said you came home, found your wife with another man, and shot him."

The officer blinked, trying to gather the words. "I what?"

It took a few minutes before the truth surfaced. He had been taking a prescription sleep aid—one known for causing vivid, realistic dreams and episodes of sleepwalking.

He had dreamed the entire thing.

He didn't remember dialing 911, didn't remember the words, and didn't even remember getting out of bed. But the call had come from his phone. His voice. Clear as day.

We stood there, the absurdity settling over us like fog. The sergeant exhaled and rubbed his temples. "Guess we found our lesson for the night."

The officer sat up, fully awake now, staring at the phone on his night-stand like it had betrayed him. "I'm done with those pills," he said quietly.

"Good idea," the sergeant replied.

When we cleared the scene, the sky was turning a faint gray—that borderland between night and morning where exhaustion feels like a second skin.

Back at the station, word spread fast. The Chief didn't find it funny, but he did find it useful. Within a week, he ordered a review of night-shift sleep issues. A month later, he released a recommendation for permanent shift assignments—day or night, no more flip-flopping every few weeks.

It changed everything.

For the first time in years, officers began to settle into a rhythm. The night owls stayed nocturnal. The early risers stuck to daylight. Fewer mistakes. Fewer near misses. A quieter kind of balance.

* * *

It was the same prescription sleep aid I had used myself to get through night shift.

That realization never needed to be spoken out loud that night, but it stayed with me all the same. Watching another officer unravel under the weight of exhaustion and medication forced a quiet recognition: this wasn't a cautionary tale about someone else. It was close. Close enough to understand how easily good intentions, chronic fatigue, and a small orange bottle could intersect in ways no one plans for and no policy anticipates.

We still joke about that night sometimes—not with mockery, but with relief. It's the kind of story you laugh about later only because you're allowed to.

Chapter 9—After the Noise

Do not waste time on what you cannot control.

—Marcus Aurelius

Quiet isn't peace. It's what's left after adrenaline burns off and no one's talking. It's the hum of the cruiser after the worst calls—the sound of what you didn't lose and what you did. After years on patrol, the calls don't stop—they thin out.

Not all at once.

At first in moments, then in stretches. At first, you think it's luck. Then you realize it's change. You start noticing things you used to tune out—the tick of the clock in roll call, the soft pop of the radio before dispatch speaks, and the hollow quiet of an empty squad room at dawn.

For years, chaos was comfort. It was the only place that made sense. The noise gave rhythm to your life, and you only felt like yourself when you were moving. Stillness never sat quite right. But now, it follows you home, sits across from you at the dinner table, and rides beside you in the car. It's strange, the first time you hear your own heartbeat. You start to wonder if this is what peace sounds like—or if it's just the echo of everything you've seen that doesn't have anywhere else to go.

That's when I realized even time away from the job isn't an ending. It's a test. Not of what you did—but of what's left when the uniform comes off. Long before I ever considered hanging up the badge, the cracks had already started—quiet moments that showed me silence wasn't a gift so much as exposure.

Quiet didn't always bring relief. Sometimes it just removed the distractions.

Echoes in the Silence

I didn't realize it until later, but for a long stretch of my career, chaos felt more familiar than calm. Movement created the illusion of safety. Noise meant purpose. Silence felt like a doorway you avoided.

Stillness never sat comfortably on my shoulders. Even on nights off, I'd catch myself scanning rooms, listening for tones, and checking the volume on the radio—anything that hinted at motion. Eventually that low gear stopped asking permission and started showing up everywhere: the hush at the dinner table, the pause when someone asked how my day went, and the ride home when nothing filled the gaps.

Then came the other kind—the silence that followed the shift and sat beside me like it had been waiting its turn. The stillness in the car before I stepped out. The quiet when I hung the uniform back in the closet. In those pauses, I realized the thoughts I'd pushed aside on busy nights hadn't gone anywhere. They were still right where I'd left them.

It's strange, the first time you hear your own heartbeat louder than the radio—stranger still when you realize you've never really listened to it before. You start wondering whether that steady thump is peace or just the residue of a thousand calls that never found a place to settle.

That was when I understood something no academy instructor ever said out loud: time away from the street isn't a reward. It's a reckoning. Without the badge, the belt, or the constant hum of calls, you're left standing in your own stillness—and stillness asks questions.

The truth is, the cracks didn't start when I handed in my gear. They formed while I was still wearing it—from moments I talked myself out of feeling and pauses I ignored because the next call was already coming.

And when the noise finally faded, all that was left was the mirror—the one quiet thing that doesn't soften anything, only reflects what you've been outrunning.

The Vacation Test

I thought distance might quiet it. I was wrong.

The first real vacation I took while I was still on patrol should've felt like freedom. It didn't. My wife and I drove to Gatlinburg, Tennessee, trading patrol lights for mountains and the hum of the town for the rustle of leaves.

No radio. No gun. No uniform. No Batman belt around my waist—just us walking hand-in-hand along the shops and cobblestone streets.

For a while, it worked. The smell of fudge and campfire smoke drifted through the air. People laughed. Kids ran past with taffy in their hands. I almost forgot what it felt like to always be scanning, always listening.

Then the sound came. Sirens.

Two cruisers screeched up beside a local bar, and before I could blink, two uniformed cops were wrestling with a man twice their size in the doorway. Chairs went flying, glass shattered, and voices shouted over each other.

The hairs on my neck rose—instinct kicking in before thought could catch up. A tiny part of me knew I should stay put, that this wasn't my jurisdiction anymore, but instinct doesn't care about state lines. Instinct moves first.

My wife's hand slipped into mine, tight. She didn't have to say a word. I knew what she meant: Don't.

But that wasn't me. That wasn't who I was.

I stepped forward, opened the door, and called out, "I'm a cop!" The words came out before I even decided to speak—my mouth moving faster than my mind could stop it. I wasn't there to play savior; I was there because muscle memory answered first.

One of the officers glanced back, wide-eyed, and I jumped in, grabbing an arm, helping to hold the man down until another officer cuffed him. The moment the cuffs clicked, the fight drained out of the room—and the adrenaline surged through me like a floodgate opening.

I stood there catching my breath, heart hammering, the air thick with sweat and beer. One of the young officers nodded, muttered a quick "Thanks," and I just smiled.

Walking back out into the sunlight, I felt it—that familiar rush, the pulse of purpose. For a moment, I was right back where I belonged. This was me. Stillness only works if the part of you that misses the noise stays asleep.

My wife didn't say a word when I rejoined her on the sidewalk. She just looked at me—that look of understanding, pride, and worry all tangled together—then took my hand again. We kept walking, the sirens fading behind us, the faint scent of campfire smoke still clinging to the air—two worlds that never stop following me.

Later, I'd learn that the tension wasn't new—it had been living under my skin for years, even when I still wore the uniform daily.

The Full Moon Shift

What followed taught me something different—that quiet doesn't always wait for permission to turn back into work.

I used to think the quiet after a long shift was something you could trust.

They say the full moon brings out the crazy. I used to laugh at that—until I worked enough of those nights to know better.

It was a Saturday shift—the kind that runs you straight into the night. The kind that starts slow, lulls you into thinking you might catch a break, and then unravels one call at a time. The moon was already hanging low and bright over the town, fat and perfect, like a spotlight witnessing everything. The radio was already on fire—domestics, bar fights, welfare checks, alarms. Every voice on dispatch sounded half an octave higher than usual.

By the time I clocked out, the sun was long gone, and the town's noise had started to thin. I headed home in my car, easing out past the edge of town onto a two-lane highway lined with pines that leaned over the road like spectators. It was quiet—the kind of quiet you earn, not trust. The kind that feels like it's waiting for you to look away. The kind that made the hairs on my arms rise even before anything happened.

Then the headlights appeared in my mirror.

A Firebird. Low, fast, and angry. It came out of nowhere, closing the distance until it was so close behind me. I could've sworn the driver was reading my VIN number off the dash. I stayed at the speed limit, hands steady on the wheel, that old familiar heat rising up the back of my neck. The shift wasn't over; it had just changed clothes. My jaw tightened on instinct, my body making decisions long before my mind caught up.

Then he swung out to pass.

The engine roared past my window, and before I could exhale, he brake-checked hard—close enough that I saw the shimmer of his taillights flash across my windshield and felt the thump of my brakes. The whole car trembled, a vibration that went straight through my ribs. Every instinct snapped awake. The distance between on-duty and off-duty vanished in a heartbeat.

Was he drunk? Or worse—someone I'd arrested, someone who still remembered my name and face?

He slowed like he might turn off, then slid right back in behind me, hugging my bumper again. I reached for the handheld radio I kept in the passenger seat and keyed up dispatch. My voice came out level, but my pulse was doing its own thing.

"Unit off duty," I said. "Possible tail, five miles outside town limits. Any deputies or troopers in the area?"

The reply came quickly. "Trooper will meet you at the Harker's Island crossroads, three minutes up the road."

"10-4," I said, keeping my eyes on the mirror.

The Firebird was still there, shadow-close, lights bouncing off my rear glass. Three minutes feels like forever when you're measuring it in taillights. I counted each dotted line like it was a fuse burning down. I stayed at the limit, counting the white lines, refusing to give him the satisfaction of a reaction.

Then the crossroads appeared—that stretch of asphalt cut by another lonely road—the trooper's car rolled out of the dark, falling in behind the Firebird.

Instant transformation. The guy in the Firebird straightened up, slowed down, and suddenly drove like a model citizen—ten-and-two on the wheel, brake lights behaving, blinker polite.

The trooper hit his blue lights. The Firebird turned into a convenience store lot, tires crunching gravel.

I pulled in a short distance away, watching the whole thing unfold under the white hum of the canopy lights. The trooper approached the driver, got the license and keys, and then walked back toward me. I recognized him immediately—we'd backed each other up on plenty of long nights.

I stepped out to meet the trooper. I saw the driver's reaction when he saw my uniform.

Priceless.

"What's the story?" he asked.

I gave him the short version—the tailgating, the brake check, the sudden act.

He nodded, jaw tightening. "He's ten sheets into the wind," he said. "I'm taking him for DWI."

I let out a slow breath I hadn't realized I was holding.

"I'll be there for court," I told him.

He smiled, tired but knowing. "Figured you would be."

As the trooper cuffed him and read the charges, the full moon hung high over the lot—pale, round, and watching. The same moon that, for reasons no one could explain, seemed to pull the crazy right up out of the ground.

Driving home later, I kept replaying the way my hands had found the wheel without thinking and the way my eyes never left the mirrors even after the road emptied. The adrenaline faded slowly, leaving that familiar hum in my chest.

The Intruder

By then, I should've known better than to trust calm simply because it showed up unannounced.

The week had been long—one of those day-shift stretches that left you both wired and exhausted. When it finally ended, I was ready for something simple. My wife had surprised me with a new smoker, and I couldn't wait to break it in. Beer-can chicken, a fire pit, and a cold beer—that was the plan. No radio. No calls. No uniform. Just us.

By dusk, the air had turned crisp. The fire cracked and spit under a full moon, the smoke curling up into the kind of night that makes you forget the noise of the world. My two-year-old was already asleep, and my wife joined me by the fire, bundled in a blanket, her face lit orange by the flames.

Whippoorwills called somewhere in the woods. The neighborhood was quiet. The kind of quiet that feels earned. I had cops on three sides: one to my right, one on the left, and two across the street. Safe. Or at least, that's what I told myself.

We sat there for hours, watching the fire shrink into a glowing bed of coals. When the last ember faded, we headed in. I remember thinking how rare that peace was. How ordinary it felt, how good.

Sleep came easy.

I don't know how long I'd been out when I heard my son's small voice in the dark.

"Mommy, I'm thirsty."

My wife got up, padded down the hall, poured him a glass of water, and tucked him back in. A few minutes later, I heard her stop in the doorway of our bedroom. Every sense sharpened at once.

She whispered, "There's someone in our yard." Her voice had that thin, trembling edge. The kind she tried to hide but couldn't. It was the kind of fear you don't mistake when you've heard it a hundred different ways on calls.

That snapped me upright. The words hit like cold water. I reached for the weapon in the holster beside the bed and chambered a round. My heart was already beating like it was back on shift. The room felt smaller, tighter. Every corner suddenly too loud.

"What did you see?" I asked, keeping my voice low.

"A man," she said. "He was standing by the window. Just… watching me."

I moved to the dining room, gun angled low. The house was dark except for the thin gray light of the moon slipping through the blinds. Every floorboard seemed to breathe under my feet.

Then she whispered again, tighter now. "He's at the end of the property—he's walking back toward the house."

I opened the back door. The night air hit cold against my skin.

"Babe," she said behind me, "you're in your underwear."

"I don't care," I told her. "Call 911."

The yard was half-shadow, half-silver. The moon had started to fade behind a streak of clouds, and that's when I saw him—about twenty-five feet out. Hoodie up, hands buried deep, just standing there. Close enough to see the lettering on his jacket.

I heard my wife on the phone. "Man in a hooded jacket. My husband's got him at gunpoint. He's an off-duty cop."

"Show me your hands!" I shouted. "Get on the ground!"

He froze, then dropped to his knees, voice cracking. "Please—please don't shoot me!"

Then his phone started ringing.

"It's my wife," he stammered. "She's wondering where I'm at. Can I answer it?"

"No!" I barked. "If you reach for that pocket, I'll shoot you!"

Then, the sound that always meant help—sirens.

A few minutes later, flashlights cut through the dark. Two deputies came around the side of the house. I stepped back inside, cleared my weapon, and pulled on pants while they took over. One of them came to the porch a few minutes later, his voice low and professional.

"He says he's your neighbor. Came to borrow firewood."

I stared past him into the yard. The man was standing now, head down, hands cuffed.

"I don't recognize him with the hood on," I said. "If that's true, send him home. I won't press charges."

Turned out, he was my neighbor—just a few houses down. I'd waved to him when he was walking around the neighborhood with his family. Shared nods across lawns. But after that night, he never walked by again.

Maybe embarrassment. Maybe fear.

For me, it was something else.

It was how fast the world could turn, even when I thought I was off the clock.

That night was supposed to be for rest. Sometimes it wasn't the calls that made you flinch—it was the quiet you mistook for safety.

The Call That Didn't Break

Not every test came in the form of danger. Some arrived quietly—and asked you to slow down instead of react.

It was late summer. The radio lit up with a domestic—third time that week at the same address. I knew the street and knew the house. The porch light always flickered, and the screen door hung crooked, like it was tired of being slammed.

When I got there, a rookie was already inside—his first week off training. His voice carried through the doorway, sharp and too loud. He was in over his head, trying to control the scene with volume instead of presence.

Inside, a man stood by the kitchen table, shirt half-torn, face red with drink. The woman was crying, pressing a towel to her arm where a glass had shattered. The rookie kept repeating himself, his hand hovering near his taser. The room smelled like sweat, spilled beer, and ashtrays—the kind of air that made tempers stick.

I didn't announce myself. I just stepped beside him and lowered my tone. "Take a breath," I whispered. "He's not swinging—he's talking. Let him talk."

The man turned toward me, chest heaving. "You cops always take her side!" he shouted.

I held his gaze and didn't answer. Sometimes silence carries more authority than words. I could feel the rookie beside me vibrating with adrenaline, waiting for anything to go wrong. He waited for me to rise to it—to meet anger with anger—but I didn't. I just stood there, still, grounded.

Top used to say, "Control the air first. If you own the air, you own the room."

Within a minute, the man's breathing slowed. His shoulders dropped. The rookie looked lost, like he was waiting for a cue.

"Let's step outside," I said finally. My voice didn't rise; it didn't need to. The man nodded, almost relieved. Outside, he sat on the steps and started crying.

Back in the cruiser a few minutes later, the rookie shook his head. "How did you know he wasn't going to fight?"

I smiled. "I didn't. But I knew I didn't have to."

That was one of those nights that never make the news—no highlight reel, no body-cam moment. But those were the calls that mattered.

As we cleared the call, I looked over at him. "You did fine," I said. "But next time—wait for backup before going in."

He started to argue, pride and adrenaline still running hot. I cut him off gently. "It's good to be eager," I told him. "But don't confuse energy with judgment. Cops get killed because they rush in before they think—or before help gets there."

He nodded, quiet now, staring into the distance, replaying it all. I let the silence stretch before adding, "The goal isn't to win fast. It's to go home."

And sometimes, the hardest part wasn't the chaos—learning to trust the quiet you create in the middle of it.

Not every test of quiet comes at home. Some come back on the street.

The Ditch Diplomats

And sometimes, the job reminded you—with mud and laughter—that control didn't always have to look serious to be real.

Midnight was quiet, but it didn't feel finished. The moon hung low over the Carolina pines, bright enough to bleach the asphalt silver. I was halfway through a lukewarm cup of gas-station coffee when dispatch crackled: "Check on a male walking in the roadway."

Sounded simple. Lonely pedestrian. Maybe a drunk, maybe someone out for a midnight stroll. The road out there runs straight for miles, lined with ditches deep enough to swallow a small car. I rolled slow, windows cracked, the smell of ocean drifting in.

Then my headlights caught movement—two shapes thrashing in the weeds.

At first, my brain filed it under possible attack. Adrenaline rose, muscle memory kicked in. I angled the cruiser across the lane, blue lights strobing, thumb hovering near the radio mic. But as the spotlight swung wide, the scene came into focus.

Not an ambush.

A wrestling match.

Between two off-duty state troopers. I recognized them immediately—jeans, T-shirts, and the unmistakable full-grown-man enthusiasm of a fight that should never have made it into adulthood.

They were rolling around in the ditch like toddlers fighting over a toy. Mud flew. Denim tore. One man's boot sailed into the road and landed with a lonely thump.

"Dispatch, I've located the subject."

Pause.

"Do you need backup?"

"Negative."

I stepped out, hand near my belt out of habit, already calculating how badly my uniform would lose if it met ditch water. Up close, the smell hit—wet leaves and stagnant water. The "fight" was almost polite. Every few seconds one of them would slur, "You're my brother, man," before trying to shove the other's face back into the mud.

"Gentlemen," I said.

They froze mid-grapple, blinking up through the beam of the spotlight like raccoons caught stealing out of a trash can. Both were ten sheets to the wind—boozy smiles, glassy eyes, and the unmistakable perfume of bad whiskey and worse decisions.

One finally croaked, "Officer... this isn't what it looks like."

"It's exactly what it looks like," I said.

They sat up, dripping and sheepish, shirts torn at the seams. These were sharp troopers—disciplined, squared-away professionals who usually looked like recruiting posters in uniform. Tonight, they looked like gravity had personally betrayed them.

One tried for dignity. "We were just play-fighting."

The other nodded solemnly. "But I was winning."

"All right," I said. "That's enough."

That did it. The moment broke. They started apologizing over each other, tripping over words the same way they'd tripped into the ditch.

I decided the night didn't need paperwork. I confiscated the half-empty bottle rolling near the curb and told them I'd be providing complimentary taxi service in a fully marked unit.

They climbed into the back seat, still arguing softly about football stats and who started it. I drove through the quiet streets, windows down, letting the night air flush out the smell of whiskey and swamp water.

Halfway home, one leaned forward, voice thick with remorse. "You're not gonna tell the first sergeant... or my wife... are you?"

I met his eyes in the mirror. "Tell them what?"

Both men exhaled at the same time.

When we reached their neighborhood, they thanked me and staggered toward the porch—muddy, laughing, and reminding me that even professionals occasionally forget how close the ditch always is.

As I pulled away, the cruiser tires hummed against the pavement, and I felt the tension finally let go.

Some calls stick because of danger.

Others stick because they remind you that control doesn't always come from force—sometimes it comes from knowing when to take the bottle, give a ride, and let the lesson last longer than the hangover.

The Routine That Wasn't

They always say there's nothing in this job that's routine—but the truth is, some days tried to rhyme.

The morning started the same way: the slow shuffle into the diner where the coffee was burnt, the bagels were cold, and the eggs were always a little too runny. But it didn't matter. The laughter and jabs across the table made it taste like home. Routine never saved us, but it softened the edges.

Sometimes breakfast doubled as roll call. The local restaurant kept us tucked in the back, away from their regular customers—maybe because our language wasn't Sunday-school friendly, or because we got a little too loud when the stories started flying. Either way, it worked. Between bites of greasy bacon and coffee refills, we hashed out the day's plan.

There was comfort in that kind of routine. You knew where you sat, who would show up late, and who'd be first to crack a joke. The conversation always bounced between serious and stupid—one minute debating call assignments, the next arguing whether gas-station biscuits were better than the diner's. Most mornings, laughter carried louder than the clatter of dishes.

We'd split up the duties—one of us walking the kids across the crosswalk at the elementary school, another shadowing the school buses to catch drivers who thought their time was worth more than a child's safety, and a few running radar in the school zones. I never minded writing a ticket for passing a stopped bus. I'd seen the near misses—the screech of brakes, the frozen faces of parents—the kind of seconds that could break a lifetime.

After the morning rush, we'd move on to the paperwork—warrants to serve, civil papers to deliver, and the endless list of things that kept the gears turning between calls. It wasn't glamorous, but it was part of the rhythm. Those small tasks filled the space between chaos and calm, between who we were and who the job expected us to be. Sometimes the clock felt like it was wading through mud, but at least it was moving.

Then came lunch—greasy pizza or cold hamburgers, whatever we could grab before the next call broke the lull. But it wasn't really about the food. It was the camaraderie—the teasing, the arguments, and the belly laughs that came from somewhere deep. It was the unspoken understanding that this might be the last meal we shared before something went sideways.

It wasn't always routine. It wasn't even close. But those quiet hours in between—those predictable, monotonous, perfectly imperfect slices of the day—that was the glue. The rhythm that held us together before the next storm rolled in. Looking back now, I realize those small hours weren't filler. They were the stitching that kept us whole.

I think that's what I missed most when the noise stopped—not the calls or the adrenaline, but the rhythm. The small, ordinary things that kept the chaos human. When you lose that, the silence doesn't feel like peace. It feels like something is missing—a song that cuts off mid-chorus.

The longer I wore the badge, the more I realized stillness could be both a gift and a test. It made you think too much. It forced you to face what you'd buried under noise. And facing it meant learning—slowly, painfully—the difference between knowing and understanding. Understanding came late, and only when the job finally went quiet enough for the truth to surface.

That truth didn't arrive all at once.

It came slowly—mile by mile—on the long road ahead.

Chapter 10—The Long Road

You think experience will hand you wisdom like a certificate—a moment where it clicks and suddenly you understand the world, the job, and yourself. But it doesn't work like that. Experience doesn't make you wise; it just gives you more to carry. The real education comes later, in the quiet moments you never thought would matter—when empathy erases judgment, when the people you once shook your head at start to look uncomfortably familiar. That's when the job stops being something you do and starts becoming something you have to face.

There's a long stretch of road between knowing better and doing better. You walk it slowly, sometimes stubbornly, collecting lessons you didn't ask for and truths you weren't ready to hear. At first, you think the job is teaching you about the danger, the chaos, and the way people come apart under pressure. But eventually, you realize it's teaching you about yourself. Every call, every mistake, every moment where fear met responsibility—all of it becomes a mirror. And that mirror doesn't soften anything.

Understanding doesn't arrive with the badge or the years. It slips in during the moments between the noise—the second you stop reacting long enough to notice the weight you've been dragging behind you. That's where the real shift begins, not in the chaos but in the calm that follows it. The day you stop sprinting toward every call just to feel useful—the day you slow down, think, and choose—that's when you realize the job's hardest lessons were never about tactics. They were about temperament, patience, and the courage to face what the silence brings.

The Calm Between Chaos

You don't notice when it happens, not really.

One day you are the rookie, racing to every call, chasing adrenaline like it's oxygen. Your voice trembles on the radio, your hands sweat on the wheel, and you pray no one else hears the shake in your voice. You tell yourself confidence will come when experience does.

But experience does not arrive all at once. It seeps in quietly, one shift, one scar, and one mistake at a time. You learn what to hold, what to let go, and how to live with what stays with you.

Top used to say, "The best officers aren't the ones who move first. They're the ones who move last, after they've thought through what everyone else missed."

Back then, I thought he was talking about tactics. Now I know he was talking about temperament.

In the beginning, I mistook speed for skill. I thought decisiveness meant being first through the door, first on the radio, and first to cuff. But every time I led with impulse, I left a mess for someone calmer to clean up. Years later, I realized what Top had known all along. The calm you bring into chaos is what separates the professional from the reckless.

There is a rhythm to good policing, and it isn't fast. It's deliberate. A measured heartbeat that steadies the people around you. The best officers don't just manage a scene; they manage emotion.

The shift from rookie to veteran doesn't happen when the calls get easier. It happens when the silence between them starts to matter. When you take that first breath before you speak, that half-second pause where clarity wins over instinct. That breath is everything. It's the difference between noise and command, between chaos and control.

Top had that quiet gravity. He never had to bark orders. He could walk into a room full of noise and people just settled. Not because they feared him, but because he carried a peace that said, I've been here before. I'm not afraid of it.

I used to wonder how he did it. Years later, I understood.

He had learned not to fight the storm.

Calm wasn't the absence of fear. It was the mastery of it.

The day I realized that, I stopped being a rookie. I started becoming someone others looked to for the same steadiness I borrowed from him.

What the Years Teach You

There's a rhythm you only find after years in uniform, something between duty and distance, noise and quiet. It doesn't come from rank or training. It comes from surviving enough nights to know that control isn't about shouting louder or moving faster. It's about standing still inside the chaos, holding your ground when everything else tilts off center. It's the stillness that settles into your bones, the part of the job that no academy syllabus ever touches.

Top used to say, "Anybody can run toward a fight. The hard part's learning when not to."

Back then, I nodded like I understood. But I didn't. Not yet. I still carried that young man's need to prove something—to the job, to the older officers, and to myself.

Years later, when rookies started calling me "sir," when the chatter on the radio sounded younger than I remembered, and the gray in my hair stopped being a surprise, that's when his words began to land. Not as advice, but as instinct. Even the gear felt different by then—the duty belt, a familiar weight instead of a burden, and the radio mic fitting into my palm like it had learned the shape of my grip.

There's a storm in every cop. You learn early how to contain it, but not how to silence it. For some, the storm burns out. For others, it settles, heavy and low, a pressure you carry until you learn how to use it. I used to think calm came from time. It doesn't. Steadiness comes from understanding—watching a hundred moments that could have gone wrong and realizing that the right word, or even the right silence, can shift everything. It's a strange skill, learning how much power lives in restraint.

After enough years, you begin to trust stillness. It's not peace. It's awareness. It's knowing the rhythm before the noise begins. You start recognizing the tone in a caller's voice before the words register, the shift in a suspect's shoulders before their feet even move.

I used to watch rookies vibrate with energy, tapping their flashlights against their legs, ready to sprint at the first sign of motion. I understood it. I'd been that way once. But eventually, you learn that patience isn't hesitation. It's control. And when you finally understand that, you realize you've crossed an invisible threshold—the point where instinct stops being reaction and starts becoming judgment.

The Night the Road Disappeared

We'd just finished a late dinner at the Chicken Shack—grease on our fingers, laughter still hanging in the air. The sort of meal that marked the calm before the storm. Summer nights had their own pulse. You could feel it building even before the first call went out.

The smell of fried food clung to our uniforms as we stepped out into the night air. A few of us leaned against patrol cars, letting the cool summer night settle in, radios clipped to our shoulders crackling with the hum of other districts. We were getting ready for what we knew would be a long stretch of back-to-back calls.

Then the tones hit.

"Trooper in chase," dispatch said, voice tight. "Eight miles outside of town."

Everything stopped. Conversations cut off mid-sentence. Every head turned toward the sound of the radio.

We could hear the dispatcher calling out road names—each one closer to our line. County Line. Marsh Road. Old Mill Road. You could feel the collective breath tighten. We all waited for the same two words: "Mutual aid."

Engines roared almost in unison. We rolled toward the edge of town and stacked up at the limits, headlights off, waiting for direction. The night felt alive—a low hum of anticipation that only cops know, the moment right before the chaos picks who it wants.

The chase lasted minutes, but it felt like an eternity. The radio chatter blurred into static and adrenaline. Then:

"Suspect wrecked off Old Mill Road. Foot pursuit in progress."

We braced, listening for the next line.

Then, "Subject in custody."

Relief came first. Then the disappointment—the kind only an adrenaline-starved night can give. I exhaled and turned down the volume, already half-expecting another call to drop.

And then it did.

"Trooper calling 10-33," dispatch said. "Emergency traffic only."

The sergeant keyed up immediately. "All units roll. Let's move."

We moved as a convoy—sirens cutting the quiet apart. The backroads flashed blue. Light bouncing off pine trees. Deputies joined. The map in my head ran through possibilities: wreck, ambush, fight, or worse.

We reached the area, but no one could find the road. Finally, a deputy spotted it—an unmarked dirt path half hidden behind overgrown brush. We turned down one by one, tires slipping on loose gravel.

At the end of that path sat chaos.

Blue lights strobed across a wide dirt lot, throwing ghostly shapes on the metal siding of a warehouse. Dozens of people were milling around—locals, whoever had come out when the sirens cut through the dark.

Then I saw him.

The trooper lay on the hood of his cruiser, shirt torn, campaign hat on the ground, his face streaked with dirt and frustration. Gun missing.

Before anyone could answer, a shotgun blast tore through the night. A deputy fired once into the air, and the crowd broke apart like a sudden storm scattering leaves. Half a dozen weapons came up, scanning the tree line and shadows.

The echo slammed into us—one hard, rolling boom that silenced everything.

For a heartbeat, no one moved. Then came the voice on the hailer, one of the deputies yelling through the loudspeaker, "This is the Sheriff's Department! Disperse immediately!"

The crowd broke apart like leaves in wind, scattering toward the dark. The trooper stood, brushing himself off, breathing hard but grinning faintly, with that look that comes when adrenaline meets embarrassment.

"What the hell happened?" the sergeant asked.

"Guy was cuffed," he said. "Next thing I know, the crowd's let him go and they picked me up and threw me on the car."

The sergeant just stared at him. "He's still cuffed?"

The trooper nodded, half-shrugging. "He didn't take 'em off."

We started searching, flashlights cutting through the brush and fields. A deputy radioed in: "Possible movement near the trailers."

We fanned out slowly. The night had gone completely still again. That eerie calm that only follows gunfire. Crickets started chirping like nothing had happened.

The deputy's voice came back: "Found him."

We rounded the corner and stopped. Through the window of a small house at the end of the road, a man sat on his couch, watching TV—hands still cuffed behind his back.

He looked up when we entered, eyes wide but calm. "Y'all took long enough," he said.

He hadn't run far. Just home.

The trooper looked at him, then at us, shaking his head. "I'll take it from here," he muttered, though we all knew this one would live forever in roll-call stories.

A procession of highway patrol cars arrived with the first sergeant leading.

We cleared the scene, the crowd gone, the noise fading until only the hum of the engines remained.

By the time we got back to town, the air had that strange hollow feeling that follows chaos—a silence too still to trust. The Chicken Shack sign still glowed faintly in the distance, the smell of grease and fried chicken mixing with cold night air.

No more calls came that night.

Just crickets. And the sound of engines cooling in the dark.

Nights like that reminded me that control isn't about calm weather, but about holding steady when the road disappears beneath you.

The Ones We Find

It started with a daughter's voice that wouldn't stop trembling. Her father had walked away from the rest home again, but this time he hadn't come back. "He gets turned around," she said over and over, like a prayer and an apology at once.

Missing-elder calls don't spike your adrenaline the way fights do. They lengthen your breath. You think in grids, not sirens. The air was cooling off when we staged at the edge of a neighborhood that backed into farmland.

Patrol units took the roads. A rookie and I walked the hedgerows with flashlights low, sweeping light across grass and ditches.

The daughter stood near her car, hands knotted in her sweatshirt. I asked for the simple things. His name. What he called her. Whether he favored a side when he walked. She said he loved baseball on the radio and the smell of cut hay. That last part mattered. People drift toward what feels familiar.

Top used to say, "Don't just search the map. Search the person." So we did.

We believed he was still close, maybe in the open fields east of the rest home. We circled slowly, lights off, windows down, calling his name through the loudhailer. The cruiser crawled along the fence line, engine barely above idle. Each time we called his name, the sound rolled out into the night, unanswered but still worth saying.

A female rookie I'd been training took the north fence. She didn't say much on the scene, but she listened like the ground itself might answer if she gave it time.

A minute later, her voice came over the air, soft but steady. "I've got something. Possible visual, northeast field, twenty yards off the fence."

We moved fast without rushing. He was there, lying on his side—cap still on, shoes muddy—breathing easy like the earth itself had told him to rest. When the flashlight found him, he blinked and tried to sit up, confused that the day had turned to night without asking his permission.

"Evening, sir," she said, kneeling so he didn't have to look up. "You gave us a walk."

He frowned, then smiled like he'd remembered the punch line. "I was headed to the ballgame," he said, looking at the field like it might still take him there.

We checked him—pulse, skin, pupils—no trauma, just distance. The daughter reached the fence line and froze, afraid to startle him with her relief. I waved her in. When he saw her, his eyebrows lifted in boyish surprise. "You found me," he said, as if she were the one who had been lost.

Back at the cars, a paramedic tucked a blanket around his legs and poured him water. No ceremony, no spotlight. Just quiet care. The daughter tried to thank everyone at once, words spilling out faster than she could shape them. We let her. Gratitude is part of the medicine.

On the way back, the rookie asked what made her check the north fence instead of the trees. I told her the truth. "She listened to the story." Baseball on the radio. The smell of cut hay. Calm isn't just a tone. It's attention.

Some calls end with headlines. The ones you keep end with a blanket, a cup of water, and a daughter's shoulders finally dropping. We don't always get to save people. Some nights, we just get to find them. And that's enough.

The Call You Don't Forget

There are moments that divide a career, not by rank or years served, but by how they rearrange something inside you.

This one came near the end of a long week, the kind where every call feels like déjà vu. Dispatch sent me to a possible suicide attempt. A young man. A note was found by his sister. No weapon mentioned. I'd worked enough of those to know what kind of quiet waited behind that door.

When I arrived, a neighbor stood on the lawn, arms folded tight, trying not to look at me. The sister sat on the steps, shaking. Inside, the house smelled like candle wax. I moved slowly, no lights, no shouting, just the deliberate calm you learn after too many scenes that start fragile and end loud.

He was sitting on the floor of his bedroom, back against the wall, a pistol beside him—something the sister must have missed or been too shaken to say. His eyes were glassy and distant but alive. I didn't say anything at first. I just eased into the doorway and waited for him to notice me.

When he finally did, he said, "Why are you here?"

"I'm here to listen," I said quietly.

For a long minute, nothing. Then his jaw trembled, his breath broke, and the words came. Heartbreak. Failure. Guilt. I didn't interrupt. I didn't reason with him. I just stayed there, anchored, letting him find his way through the storm.

Top used to say we had to be masters of the craft—ready to wear whatever hat the moment demanded. Cop. Counselor. Anchor. Whatever the person in front of you needed most. And in the hardest moments, he warned us not to turn inward. This isn't about you, he'd say. Learn how to carry what people place in your hands without making it your own.

Top once told me, "You can't outtalk pain. You just have to outlast it."

Eventually, he slid the pistol toward me. We sat there until paramedics arrived. Later that night, after the paperwork, the rookie who rode backup asked, "What did you say to him to make him give it up?"

"Nothing," I said. "Sometimes silence says enough."

It took me years to learn that lesson. Strength doesn't always shout. Sometimes it just stays.

The Cost of Calm

There was a stretch when I couldn't turn the job off. Even in bed, my body waited for the next tone, the next voice over the radio. My wife used to joke that I carried police work in my bloodstream. She wasn't wrong.

The job rewires you. You start scanning rooms without realizing it, sitting with your back to walls, mapping exits. It isn't paranoia. It's survival learned by repetition. But after enough years, you begin to wonder what's left that isn't trained.

That's when Top's lesson took root. Don't chase calm. Make it.

I started doing small things differently. Sitting in silence before shift. Standing outside after a call until my breath slowed. I didn't call it meditation. I called it maintenance.

Even then, calm came at a cost. You carry it long enough, and it starts to weigh. Sometimes you're steady. Sometimes you're numb. The line between composure and detachment blurs.

It broke one summer after two back-to-back funerals. Both officers were younger than I was. Both died doing things I once did without hesitation. I'd been the calm one for everyone else. Suddenly, I couldn't find it for myself.

For weeks, I sat in my cruiser before shift, staring at the dash. The chatter on the radio felt younger and faster. I snapped at dispatchers. Barked at rookies. Even the static set my teeth on edge.

One night, my wife met me at the door. "You're not here anymore," she said. "Even when you are."

That hit harder than any call ever could.

The next morning, I drove to the edge of town, to the same road where Top used to park and watch traffic. I rolled down the window and listened. Crickets. Distant engines. Nothing else. I didn't reach for the radio or check my phone. I just let the quiet work its way back in.

I thought about all the times I'd told others to breathe. To stay human. I had forgotten to take my own advice.

That's the truth they don't teach at the academy. The job doesn't always break you. It bends you. It tests whether you can remember who you were before the badge started talking louder than your heartbeat.

Because you can't keep giving calm to everyone else if you never stop to refill it.

* * *

There comes a moment in your career when you realize you've become someone else's Top. You don't notice it at first. Someone lingers after roll call with a question. Someone calls you off duty to ask what you'd do. Someone quotes you back to yourself.

At first it's humbling. Then it's terrifying.

Because now every reaction, every pause, and every decision is a lesson someone else is learning from. You stop thinking only about how to handle calls and start thinking about how you're seen handling them.

But in that pressure, there's grace. It keeps you honest. It forces you to live the example you preach.

One of my proudest moments wasn't an award or a big case. It was walking into the break room and hearing a rookie tell another officer, "He's not fast to talk, but when he does, you listen."

It reminded me of Top. And I realized that's how legacies really pass on. Not through medals or commendations, but through the way one person teaches another to stay steady when things tilt.

After a tense domestic with an armed suspect, a young officer asked me, "You didn't even draw your gun. Weren't you scared?"

"Every time," I said. "Fear's just information. You learn to listen without obeying it."

He nodded like he understood. But I knew it would take him a few years. We all think courage is the absence of fear. It isn't. It's holding fear steady until it stops shaking your hands.

That became my mission in those final years. Not to make rookies fearless, but to teach them how to carry fear with grace. How to breathe in the storm without letting it become them.

There's no graduation for that lesson. You learn it one call at a time, one mistake at a time, one long night at a time.

The Quiet Between Beats

Sometimes I still wake before dawn, half-expecting the radio to crackle to life. Old habits don't retire. They just sleep lighter. Even now, after years on the job, my body still pauses at the same hour shift change used to hit, listening for tones that may or may not come. I lie there for a moment, feeling that old muscle memory twitch—the way vigilance lingers even when nothing is moving yet.

Eventually, I get up. I sit at the window and watch the world blink awake. A jogger passes by with steady breath and soft footfalls. A garbage truck hums down the street, its hydraulic arms clanking in a rhythm that once blended into my background noise. Somewhere a porch light clicks off; somewhere else a dog barks at the morning like it's announcing roll call. The town exhales, stretching itself back into motion, unaware of how quiet this hour used to feel when I wore a badge.

And I think of the rookies out there now. The ones sitting in parking lots between calls, watching taillights fade, wondering if they're making a difference. The ones fighting sleep at four in the morning, praying for sunrise because the silence feels heavier than the noise. I hope they know the truth—that they matter long before they realize they do.

Because they are making a difference.

Every quiet act of restraint.

Every moment of empathy that cuts through anger.

Every time they choose patience over pride.

Those moments don't earn medals. They don't make headlines. But they keep families intact, de-escalate storms, and change lives more than any arrest ever could. That's the job. That's the legacy. Not the big calls—the quiet choices no one sees.

Some mornings, as I sip my coffee and watch the sun edge over rooftops, I think about the ones still climbing the long road between knowing and understanding. I remember how many times calm didn't come naturally to me—how often I had to force it, breathe it, fake it until the moment shifted and I could genuinely feel it settle in. If they're out there struggling with the same, that's alright. Growth in this job rarely feels graceful.

The stillness isn't the absence of the storm.

It's the proof you've learned to live inside it and still find your way home.

Top used to say, "You don't stop the storm. You stand inside it."

Back then, I heard it.

Now I understand it.

Some mornings, before the house fully wakes, I notice the small things that surround the job. The radio mic rests silent on the counter, waiting. My boots are by the door, polished out of habit, ready whether I am or not. The hook in the closet where my duty belt hangs between shifts, heavy even when it's empty. The job isn't calling in that moment—but its shape is still there, woven into the rhythm of the house and the way I move through it.

And the older I get, the more I realize that what stays after the noise isn't silence at all.

It's the echoes that stayed.

Chapter 11—When the Echo Settles In

He who fears death will never do anything worthy of a man who is alive.

—Seneca

The first time you repeat your mentor's words, you realize time has moved you into their seat. You don't plan it—it just happens. One day you're the rookie gripping the wheel, mistakes still clinging to your voice. The next, you hear your own tone steadying someone younger or less experienced, and it sounds like a man you once followed through chaos without question. The shift doesn't announce itself. It settles quietly into your cadence long before you understand what it means.

I didn't recognize the transition at first. It showed up in small ways—the calmer breath before a call, the softer voice in a hallway, and the instinct to listen before speaking. I told myself it was experience, nothing more. Just years of doing the job the way it demanded. Then one night, standing in a hallway with a rookie whose hands wouldn't stop shaking, the words came out of me before I could stop them.

"Slow down. Breathe. Think first."

The words left my mouth before I realized they weren't mine.

A rookie stood in front of me, report half-finished, adrenaline still leaking from his voice. He'd just cleared his first real fight—the kind that leaves your hands buzzing long after the noise dies down. I meant to reassure him, maybe tell him he'd done fine. But what came out was instruction. Familiar. Measured. Unmistakable.

Top's instruction.

The same phrase he gave me when I was the one trying to hold still after the world came unglued.

He nodded, gripping his pen like a lifeline. His breathing slowed. His shoulders dropped a fraction. Somewhere between that alley and this hallway, something had shifted. I felt it even if I couldn't yet name it.

It hadn't happened all at once. It never does. It came from years of calls survived, lessons absorbed, and nights replayed until they stopped burning. All the quiet truths handed to me in fragments—a sentence here, a look there—had finally settled into place. And now they were coming out of my own mouth, aimed forward.

I could almost hear Top's voice layered over mine—steady, unhurried, carrying the kind of calm that doesn't need to explain itself. It wasn't haunting. It wasn't imitation. It was something passed down and carried forward.

That was when I understood what a career leaves behind.

Not arrests.

Not stories.

But echoes—steady enough to guide someone else through the noise.

When the Voice Becomes Yours

The radio clicked once in the quiet, then went still again.

We were parked behind a row of dark storefronts, the kind of place where sound carries farther than it should. Sodium lights hummed overhead. The rookie shifted in the passenger seat, adjusting his vest for the third time in a minute, then tapping his pen against his notepad like it might keep time for his breathing.

"Dispatch says he's still inside," the rookie said, too fast. "Neighbors called again. Yelling, maybe throwing things. No weapon mentioned, but—"

"But," I said gently, and let the word hang.

He stopped talking. Looked at me.

I could see it on him—the adrenaline, the need to do something. I remembered that feeling. How silence used to feel like failure.

We stepped out together. The night air was thick and warm, carrying the smell of cut grass. A porch light burned halfway down the block. Somewhere behind the house, a television blared. Voices rose and fell inside—sharp, emotional, not yet violent but close enough to taste.

The rookie's hand hovered near his radio mic.

"Slow it down," I said, barely louder than the hum of the lights. "We've got time."

He nodded, though his foot still bounced once before he caught it.

Inside, the hallway was narrow. Family photos crowded the walls—school pictures and a wedding portrait tilted slightly off center. A woman stood near the kitchen doorway, arms wrapped around herself, eyes darting between us and the closed bedroom door at the end of the hall.

"He's been like this all night," she whispered. "He won't listen."

From behind the door came a muffled shout, then silence.

The rookie took a step forward.

I didn't stop him with a command. I didn't raise my voice. I just lifted a hand—palm down—and took a breath slow enough that he noticed it.

He matched it without realizing he had.

We stood there for a moment longer than felt comfortable. Long enough for the house to settle. Long enough for the noise to lose its edge.

When the door finally opened, the man inside didn't charge or shout. He just stood there, shoulders tight, eyes red, breathing hard like he'd run out of words before he ran out of anger.

"What?" he said.

I didn't answer right away.

I watched his hands. His stance. The way his weight shifted back when he saw the uniforms. Fear hiding under the bluster.

"It's been a long night," I said. "For everyone."

His jaw worked. He looked past me, then back again. The moment teetered.

The rookie stayed quiet.

A minute later, the man sat down. The woman's shoulders dropped. The hallway felt wider somehow, like the walls had stepped back.

When we walked out, the rookie exhaled hard, like he'd been holding it since the car.

"I thought he was about to lose it," he said. "I almost jumped in."

"I know," I said.

He hesitated. "How did you know to wait?"

I opened my mouth to answer—and stopped.

Because the words that came out weren't mine.

"Slow down. Breathe. Think first."

They landed between us, solid and familiar.

He nodded, gripping his pen like it might anchor him if the ground shifted again. And standing there under the flickering light, I felt it—the quiet, unmistakable shift.

I wasn't remembering what to say.

I was carrying it.

Later, back in the car, the radio stayed silent as we pulled away. The rookie adjusted his vest once more, then left it alone. His breathing had found a steadier rhythm.

I watched the streetlights pass and understood something I hadn't before.

The voice I followed through chaos hadn't disappeared.

It had learned how to travel.

Lessons Worth Keeping

Rookies arrive like a storm: wide-eyed, loud, and certain they're invincible.

They don't yet understand that survival isn't speed—it's patience.

That's where I come in.

My job is simple on paper: train them, test them, and sign them off.

The real job is quieter—making sure they learn enough to keep breathing, to think when fear tries to think for them, and to go home to their families when the shift ends.

I used to chase every call like it owed me proof. Now I chase understanding.

At the range, I teach them how to breathe between heartbeats.

On the street, I show them how silence can settle a scene faster than any barked order.

And when one freezes or fumbles, I don't lecture; I let the stillness teach.

That's how Top did it.

He never raised his voice. Never filled the air just to fill it.

He taught me that control isn't loud—it's consistent.

Now I watch rookies make the same mistakes I once did, and I meet them with the patience he gave me.

Show, don't tell—the oldest method in the book, and still the one that sticks.

Sometimes watching them brings back how fragile we all were in those first years—the shaky hands after a fight, the laughter that came too loud after something almost went wrong, and the quiet that settled when the adrenaline left. I see the same flicker in their eyes I once carried: equal parts pride and disbelief that the world didn't end when the sirens did.

There's a strange beauty in that uncertainty. It's proof of life, proof that their empathy hasn't yet been buried under procedure. When they ask endless questions—about tactics, about fear, about why their chest still tightens hours after a call—I answer with stories, not sermons. I tell them about the first time my knees shook so hard I couldn't feel the ground, and about the way Top stood beside me, hands folded, saying nothing until my breath found me again. That's mentorship—the transfer of steadiness through presence, not performance.

And that's when I remember Top's quiet gravity.

He didn't just train me for the job; he trained me for everything that comes after it—the long hours, the weight of choices that never make reports, and the responsibility of teaching others the lesson we learned.

The Range

One afternoon, a rookie missed every target he fired at.

Frustration tightened his shoulders, each miss louder than the last.

I walked up beside him. "Stop shooting. Look at the paper."

He blinked. "What am I looking for?"

"Patterns," I said. "Even mistakes tell you what you're doing."

We started over from the ground up.

"Feet shoulder-width. Knees soft. Elbows relaxed," I said. "Grip the pistol, but don't choke it. Let it sit in your hands the way you'd hold a bird—firm enough to control it, not so tight you kill it."

He adjusted. I watched his breathing, short and shallow—the kind that pulls the sights off target before the shot ever breaks.

"Breathe in. Let half of it out. Hold it there. Now find your front sight—not the target, not the rear sight. That orange blade is your truth."

He focused. His shoulders dropped.

"Don't slap the trigger," I said quietly. "Let it surprise you. If the gun scares you when it goes off, you did it right."

He squeezed, slow and steady, until the pistol barked.

The hole appeared closer to the center. He tried again. Closer still.

"That's it," I said. "You're not forcing the shot. You're letting it happen."

He lowered the weapon and exhaled a laugh that sounded like relief.

That was the same look I'd given Top years ago when he taught me the same thing.

It wasn't just about marksmanship. It was about patience.

You don't fix chaos by adding more speed; you fix it by finding rhythm.

Top used to say, "Don't teach them to shoot. Teach them to aim."

Now I understood what he really meant—aim your mind before your weapon.

Sometimes I think of that lesson outside the range, at scenes lit by flashing blue, where tension hums like static in the air. The target changes—it's not paper anymore, it's people—but the principle is the same. You can't see straight if you're shaking inside.

The smell of cordite and sweat lingers on every range, but the lesson follows us into patrol cars and living rooms, alleyways and accident scenes. I remind them that accuracy starts long before the trigger press—in the mind that refuses to rush. Some understand it that day; others take years. I tell them that a calm shot is a promise—to the public, to your partner, and to yourself. Every bullet you control is one less regret you'll have to carry. And somewhere deep down, I still tell myself the same thing: aim small, think wide. The target is everything and nothing all at once.

The Long Game

Training rookies is not just a duty; it's a responsibility that travels home with you.

I carry their names like chapters in a book I'm still writing.

When they're nervous, I remember my own first nights.

When they are steady, I feel pride that has nothing to do with ego.

I tell each of them the same thing: "You are not here to be fearless. You are here to be ready."

They nod, half-understanding.

It will take years before those words earn their meaning.

Sometimes they ask what I want out of them.

I tell them the truth.

"I want you to make it to the end of every shift. I want you to go home to your family in one piece. That is success."

They usually smile, thinking I'm oversimplifying.

But every officer learns eventually—the real test of a night's work is not how many arrests you make; it's whether everyone gets to see tomorrow.

You stop counting wins by numbers and start counting them by mornings.

It's a strange evolution, realizing that the scoreboard doesn't matter. The victories that shape you are invisible—a child comforted, a crisis diffused, a fellow officer spared from a bad decision because someone took a breath first. Those aren't written in ink. They live in memory. When I drive home after a long shift, I roll down the window and let the air hit my face, replaying each near miss. I used to crave closure; now I crave understanding. The job isn't about chasing danger—it's about guiding it quietly toward stillness. That's what Top did for me. That's what I try to do for them.

The Rookie Mistakes

Every rookie carries a moment they wish they could take back—and every trainer carries the memory of watching them learn it the hard way.

There are funny moments too—the kind that keep you human.

A rookie locks the keys in the cruiser with the lights still flashing.

Another accidentally keys the mic while singing along to a country song.

Those mistakes are proof of growth, not failure.

I laugh with them, not at them, because Top once laughed with me when I thought the world was ending over a radio error.

He taught me that humility is part of confidence; you cannot have one without the other.

So I show them.

Show how to use tone to calm a scene.

Show how to back away without losing authority.

Show how to listen when everyone else is yelling.

And in the showing, I keep learning too.

Each time they falter, I remember the blur of my own missteps and the quiet patience of a man who once stood where I do now.

Humor saves us. It bridges the impossible gap between tragedy and endurance.

Once, an officer I knew received a complaint from a bystander who said he and his partner were laughing in public after a call. The complaint said it looked "unprofessional." What that person didn't see—or couldn't understand—was that just minutes earlier, they'd cleared an accident where a child had been killed. Their cruiser still smelled faintly of gasoline and cold night air. The laughter wasn't disrespectful. It was release—the only way to stop the grief from swallowing them whole.

A shared laugh after a long call resets the heart in ways medicine can't. Sometimes the laughter is desperate, sometimes joyful, but it always means we're still here.

I tell rookies never to lose that—the ability to laugh without cruelty, to find levity even when the night has claws.

The day you stop laughing, you start hardening. And once you harden, compassion cracks.

So we joke, not to forget, but to remember that we're still capable of happiness.

Steady the World

We were dispatched to a larceny call at the grocery store.

The clerk told dispatch the suspect had run off with two hundred dollars' worth of steaks—arms full of ribeye and sirloin steaks, Christmas week.

When we arrived, he was already cutting through the parking lot toward the tree line behind the store. My rookie was halfway out of the car before I said a word.

"What do you think?" I asked.

He pointed toward the woods. "We go in there and find him."

I shook my head. "No. A lot of cops get killed chasing people into the dark. Nobody's going to hear you scream for help out there. Let's call for a K-9."

He exhaled—a quick flash of disappointment tightening his jaw—but keyed up dispatch without arguing.

Within minutes, the handler arrived. The dog picked up the trail easily, nose low, tail stiff, weaving through the pines. Cold air carried the sharp scent of sap and old leaves, each step crunching under our boots until the dog stopped at a patch of straw.

The suspect was lying there, half-buried in pine straw, breathing hard, eyes wide. We cuffed him without incident.

Back at the car, the rookie crouched beside him. "Why'd you steal?"

The man looked down at his hands. "It's for my family. We don't have anything to eat. Christmas is coming up."

He didn't make excuses. His shoulders sagged in a way that told me he wasn't acting—the kind of defeat that settles into a person's voice when the truth is the only thing left.

We booked him, finished the paperwork, and the rookie asked, "Can we go back to the store?"

"Why?" I asked.

"I want to pay for the steaks," he said.

So we did. The manager's eyes softened when he realized what the rookie was doing. He paid for the meat out of his own pocket, tucked the bag into the back seat, and asked me to swing by the suspect's address.

The neighborhood was still—a couple porch lights glowing, cold air hanging still—the kind of place where small mercies matter.

We dropped the steaks off—no words, no announcement. Just an act that didn't need witnesses.

I sat there for a moment, watching the rookie climb back into the cruiser. The lights from the neighborhood blinked across the windshield—Christmas decorations glowing against the dark.

I'd meant to teach him about tactics that night—how to stay alive, how to use the dog, and how to control a scene.

Instead, he taught me something else.

That policing isn't just about the arrest. It's about knowing when to hold the line and when to bend the knee toward mercy.

That night, I realized the rookie didn't just steady a scene. He steadied the world—one small corner of it, for one family, and maybe for me too.

Quiet Victories

The best nights aren't the ones that make reports.

They're the ones when a rookie handles a call perfectly—de-escalation smooth, communication clean—and you don't have to step in at all.

You sit back in the cruiser, listening to the radio, and realize the lesson landed.

Top's words now live through someone you trained.

That is legacy, the quiet kind.

It doesn't earn headlines or medals. It earns peace of mind.

I don't need plaques. I need to know they're safe, that they're going home to kiss their kids goodnight. That knowledge is the only reward that matters, the one that keeps the badge from feeling light enough to lift but not so heavy it crushes you.

Sometimes, when a rookie clears a scene with that steady tone that settles the whole room, I catch myself smiling without meaning to. Not proud in the boastful sense, but proud in the way a parent watches a child finally balance on their own two feet. You see the shift happen—that moment when fear stops driving them and judgment takes its place. They don't notice it, but you do. You hear it in their voice: the way the pitch evens out, the hesitation disappears, and the urgency becomes measured instead of frantic. It's the sound of someone stepping into their own ability.

I've watched rookies grow in ways they never see in themselves. I've seen the tentative kid who once shook writing his first report turn into the officer who steps between a screaming couple and speaks so gently the whole room changes temperature. I've watched officers who once chased everything that moved learn the power of standing still. Top used to say, "Stillness is a tactic too," and I hear that echo now when I see a rookie take a breath before speaking.

There's a moment when they come back to the patrol car after handling a call—breath steady, shoulders level, eyes no longer darting. They slide into the seat, close the door, and for the first time, they don't look at you for approval. They already know.

Those nights stay with me.

More than the chases.

More than the chaos.

Because they prove the work matters—the teaching, the patience, the hours spent repeating the same phrases with the hope that one day they'll become instinct.

Sometimes I park under a streetlight after a long shift and just watch the town breathe—storefront lights blinking out, cars drifting by, the ordinary rhythm of safety returning. A breeze moves just enough to carry the wet scent of cooling asphalt, the kind you only notice at the end of a long shift. Somewhere, a siren fades until it's swallowed by the quiet. What never makes a report are the small, invisible decisions that hold a night together—the gentle word that steadied someone, the extra breath taken instead of rushing, and the simple act of listening before acting.

Quiet victories don't show up on dashboards or monthly stats. You won't find them on a spreadsheet. But they live in the spaces between calls—in the stillness after chaos, in the exhale that follows tension, and in the gratitude you feel when your whole shift goes home in the same number that started it.

People think policing is defined by the big moments—the foot pursuits, the fights, and the sirens tearing through the dark. But what shapes a career and what shapes a person are these quiet victories. The ones no one claps for. The ones that make it home without fanfare.

The real measure of success is the absence of tragedy.

Most nights, if we've done it right, the world never realizes how close it came.

I think Top would agree—our job isn't to be remembered; it's to make sure others get to forget the danger we held at bay.

Top's Echo and the Mirror

Sometimes, when the streets are quiet and the light falls just right, I feel him beside me.

Not haunting. Guiding.

It's strange how memory changes as you age in this job. Early on, you hold every moment like a sharp object—the shouts, the mistakes, the adrenaline, the blur. You cling to them because you think each one defines you. But years later, what remains isn't the noise. It's the influence—the lessons that stopped being advice and became instinct. I think that's why Top's presence feels closest during the quiet moments: memory needs stillness to speak.

There are nights when I replay the early years—the times my voice trembled on the radio, when my hands shook after clearing a house, and when fear pushed me faster than judgment ever could. I still remember the first time Top told me to slow down; that calm wasn't gifted, it was practiced. I didn't understand him then. I thought patience was something you earned after surviving enough calls. Now I know it's something you build in the in-between hours—the long drives back from scenes, the moments alone in a cruiser when the only sound is your own breath, the nights when you learn to sit with your thoughts without letting them own you.

Some of Top's lessons didn't land until years later. I hear them now in situations he never lived to see—in the quiet after a near miss, in the heaviness that settles after a fatal crash, and in the subtle shift in a rookie's voice when courage starts replacing fear. That's the thing about real mentorship: the teaching outlasts the teacher.

I tell rookies the badge isn't armor. It's accountability. Every choice they make echoes into someone else's life—and their own. They nod like they understand, but I can see in their eyes they're still learning the weight of it. I was the same. There's a moment in every officer's career when the badge stops feeling like permission and starts feeling like responsibility. You don't forget that shift. It stays with you long after the calls fade.

I sense Top most on the nights when nothing happens—when the town settles and the world feels caught up on its breath. His echo lives in unexpected places: the radio crackle before a call, the quiet between dispatch tones, and the stillness of dawn after a night that could have gone worse. Those were the moments he valued. Not the chaos. The clarity.

I catch myself repeating his phrases in other moments, too—at home with my kids, during a conversation with someone struggling at a community event, and even when I'm alone in the car sorting through the pieces of the day. His voice doesn't interrupt; it steadies.

That's legacy.

It's not marble or medals—it's the steady thread of conscience that outlasts the uniform.

Sometimes, when I catch my reflection in a window or mirror, I see him there—not the man himself, but what he left behind. The patience. The steadiness. The calm that once belonged to someone else but now lives in me. And in those moments I realize the part they don't prepare you for—that you spend a career trying to live up to someone else's example, and one day you wake up and realize you've become its continuation.

The echo becomes instinct.

The student becomes responsible for what comes next.

That's how the job carries on—not through titles or rank, but through reflection. Through the quiet passing of courage and restraint from one set of hands to the next. Through the moments when someone else steadies their breath because of something you once said or something you once learned from a man named Top.

*   *   *

There are times—usually when the radio goes quiet and the night feels unusually settled—when you realize the lessons you've been following have carried you as far as they can. Not because they've failed you, but because they've done their work. What once had to be remembered has become instinct. What once steadied you is now steadying others.

I had passed those lessons on—without ceremony, without naming them—to rookies who no longer needed me hovering nearby. I could hear it in their voices now: the pause before action, the even tone, and the restraint that didn't ask for permission. The handoff had already happened.

That realization didn't feel like loss.

It felt like completion.

The shift came on an ordinary night.

I pulled into the driveway after a late tour and shut the engine off, but I didn't get out. The house was dark except for a soft glow in the kitchen window. Inside, my family was asleep. The world I'd spent years running toward was already at rest.

I sat there with my hands on the wheel, listening to the tick of the cooling engine. The radio was still. Not dead—just waiting. I knew if I keyed it, the night would answer. It always did.

Instead, I reached up and unhooked the mic.

I set it on the console and let it stay there.

That was the moment. Not dramatic. Not final. Just honest.

* * *

I thought about the rookies I'd trained who no longer needed correction—only space. I thought about the classes I was taking at night and the way learning had begun to feel expansive instead of urgent. I thought about how the job had given me exactly what it promised—purpose, brotherhood, a way to steady chaos—and how it had quietly prepared me for something beyond the perimeter of a patrol shift.

What surprised me wasn't fatigue.

It was clarity.

I wasn't running from the work.

I was moving toward the life it had made possible.

Inside the house, textbooks were spread across the table, margins crowded with notes. Concepts I'd practiced for years now had names: communication under pressure, decision-making, and leadership without force. I recognized them immediately—not as theory, but as lived experience finally given shape.

That's when I understood the difference between leaving and carrying forward.

What Top gave me was never meant to stay locked inside a cruiser. It was meant to travel—into classrooms, conversations, and places where the radio didn't dictate the tempo. Places where steadiness could multiply instead of being spent one call at a time.

I opened the car door and stepped out into the quiet.

I knew, with a certainty I trusted, that the next stretch of road wouldn't begin with a siren. It would begin with a choice.

And I was already walking toward it.

Night School

Somewhere between teaching rookies and trying to keep up with my own lessons, I realized how much I'd stopped learning for myself.

I decided to finish the degree I'd started years before. Working shifts and studying left little room for sleep, but the classroom opened something I'd forgotten—learning for curiosity's sake.

The courses were about communication, leadership, and psychology—how people think, how they change, and how they learn. I saw the same principles in both worlds: clarity under pressure, empathy as strategy, and the discipline of listening without judgment.

One night the professor talked about experiential teaching. I smiled. That was exactly what Top had done. He never told me what to think; he let me discover it by doing.

That became my rule: don't lecture. Demonstrate.

Let them see calm instead of hearing about it.

Teaching and policing overlap. Both rely on trust. Both demand presence. Both require knowing when to speak and when to stay quiet so others can find their footing.

When I left class late those nights, the parking lot lights painted long shadows across the asphalt. The campus was quiet—no radios, no static, no chaos. Just silence. It reminded me that learning never really ends, not if you stay open to it.

Sometimes I drove straight from class to the station, textbooks still on the passenger seat beside my duty belt. The contrast was absurd—philosophy notes and arrest reports, psychology theories and radio codes—but the lessons intertwined.

Understanding human behavior in theory made me better at reading it in real time. I started recognizing fear disguised as anger and grief masked as defiance. The classroom didn't pull me away from policing; it refined how I did it.

In the quiet hum of fluorescent lights, I rediscovered curiosity.

And curiosity kept me human.

I didn't go inside right away.

I stood in the driveway a moment longer, listening to the household in its sleep—the kind of peace you don't notice until you've spent years chasing noise. The kitchen light was still on. Textbooks lay open on the table like a second kind of duty.

The choice wasn't about walking away.

It was about walking forward on purpose—toward my family, toward finishing what I'd started, toward building something steadier than a shift could promise.

The work wasn't ending.

It was widening.

Chapter 12—The Turn Toward What's Next

First say to yourself what you would be; then do what you have to do.

—Epictetus

The transition out of the job didn't happen with a ceremony or a final call.

It happened one morning when I stood in my driveway longer than necessary, keys in my hand, nowhere I had to be.

The world kept moving, but for the first time in years my pace was my own—no longer dictated by tones, dispatch, or the next crisis waiting beyond the headlights. With that freedom came something unexpected: drift. Purpose had always arrived as a radio call, and without it, the day felt wider than I expected.

At first, the silence felt like possibility. Then it started asking questions.

Quiet presses into the places you've ignored—the ones noise used to protect you from. Leaving the badge behind didn't mean leaving the lessons behind. They followed me—not as ghosts, but as guideposts.

I began to realize something I'd never slowed down long enough to notice: life after the badge isn't an ending at all. It's the same road, just with different signs and fewer sirens. The instincts forged in chaos don't disappear; they settle, and they start shaping who you are outside the uniform.

What comes next isn't a break from the job, but the part of life that proves what the job built in you.

A Sport for the Young

Policing had changed over the years, and so had I.

The rookies coming in now grew up on technology—body cams, drones, and digital evidence that moved faster than paper ever did. They carried a speed I remembered having, and watching them reminded me what it felt like to run on pure nerve.

I could still hold my own, but recovery took longer. The aches didn't scare me; they just told the truth.

The real shift wasn't my body. It was my awareness.

When I was young, I felt everything in my chest first—fear, pride, anger. With time, the focus drifted outward, where it belonged. I stopped reacting to what was happening inside me and started reading what was unfolding around me.

Top used to say, "If you feel it in your heart, you're looking inward. If you want to survive, look outward."

He wasn't wrong.

Some nights I'd stand beside a rookie under a buzzing streetlight and see the scene two ways at once—who I was then, and who I'd become. They rushed in with urgency I once mistook for courage, and I recognized the lesson I learned the hard way: adrenaline teaches fast, but consequences teach longer.

I wasn't bitter. The job is meant for the next wave—the ones who run toward the noise before they understand how close danger can get. My turn had become helping them grow into that courage, passing along steadiness that saved me more times than I could admit.

I saw pieces of myself in them—curiosity, restlessness, and the need to prove something. But I also saw a fork in the road, because they were climbing into a life I had already lived.

There comes a moment when you stop racing to keep pace with the job and start preparing those who will take your place. Standing in the glow of blue lights, watching rookies sprint toward the same chaos I once chased without hesitation, I could feel the shift.

Not resignation. Not regret.

Just recognition.

Policing begins as a sport for the young and becomes a calling for the seasoned. And once you've become the steady voice, you start hearing another one too—the one asking what your steadiness is meant to build next.

The Birth That Changed Everything

When my son was born, the world tilted.

He was small enough to fit in one hand, furious at the light, and he changed every calculation I'd ever made about time and risk. I'd spent years thinking about the safety of strangers—victims, partners, people I'd never meet again. Suddenly, my focus narrowed to one tiny heartbeat sleeping beside me.

Fear wasn't a threat anymore; it was a responsibility.

Fatherhood doesn't erase the job. It reframes it.

After shift, I'd stand in the doorway of his room and listen to him breathe. His chest rose and fell with the steady rhythm of a life untouched by what I'd seen. And for the first time in my career, I felt a pull I couldn't ignore—not away from the work, but toward him.

Daycare costs hit like the punchline to an expensive joke. I remember staring at the numbers and laughing once, quietly, because it was either laugh or feel the panic rise. But beneath the math was something deeper—the realization that the best of what the job gave me might be meant for my family now, not only for rookies and partners.

Being present started to feel like a responsibility, not a luxury.

When you work nights long enough, you measure family time in leftovers and mornings that begin as everyone else is heading out the door. I missed birthdays, barbecues, and fireworks. One Christmas morning, I called home from a gas station parking lot between calls and listened to my son open a present while a drunk argued with his reflection behind me.

I told myself it was part of the job—necessary, noble, and unavoidable. But even necessary things can cost more than you realize in the moment.

I started praying in small, plain sentences. Not bargains, not speeches—just honesty.

Lord, help me be wise. Help me be present. Help me lead my family the way I lead on the street.

When the Horizon Shifted

Twenty years.

That's how long it took for the job to feel like muscle memory—and for life outside of it to start whispering that there might be more.

I still remember walking into roll call one morning: same coffee, same jokes, same familiar rhythm. Nothing monumental happened. But somewhere between clipping my radio on and taking my seat, a quiet truth settled in—I was closing a season I didn't realize had been preparing me for its own turning.

I loved the work. Even the hard parts. Especially the hard parts, because the work mattered. It gave me purpose, identity, and a brotherhood I'd die for. The math used to feel simple: hear the noise, run toward it, hold the line.

But around the time my son was born, my horizon widened. Not because I stopped loving the job. Not because the job failed me. Because a new responsibility showed up at home, and it deserved the same seriousness I gave the street.

For the first time, I started thinking not just about the shift ahead, but the years ahead. I didn't want to drift into the next chapter. I wanted to choose it.

And once I admitted that, the next question arrived like an honest report you can't rewrite: what does a cop become when the uniform isn't doing the introductions?

For most of my adult life, the badge answered that question before I ever could.

Now I had to answer it with my own name.

The Long Way Across

I didn't cross the bridge by burning anything down behind me.

I crossed it the same way I'd crossed most things in my life—by showing up early, listening first, and accepting that I was going to be new at something again.

I decided to keep going.

Not drifting. Not dabbling. Going.

Advanced degrees. Night classes. The long road instead of the shortcut.

Walking into that first classroom felt uncomfortably familiar. Rows of desks. Fluorescent lights buzzing just enough to notice. People scanning the room, trying to place themselves. I recognized the posture immediately—the half-confidence, half-uncertainty that comes from stepping into something that matters. It felt like rookie school all over again, just without the buzz cuts and push-ups.

We were a mix of older adults. Some are chasing a second life. Some rebuilding after the first one didn't turn out the way they planned. A few were fresh out of undergrad, still carrying the speed of youth. Most of us sat somewhere in between—people who knew enough to be dangerous and enough to be humble.

Degrees on the wall promised things we all understood without saying out loud: stability, credibility, and leverage. A life less dependent on overtime and luck. A future that didn't ask your knees how long you could keep going.

I was older than most of my classmates. I didn't try to hide it. I'd already learned that pretending not to know something is more exhausting than admitting you're still learning. When professors asked questions, I didn't rush to answer. I listened. I waited. The habit followed me from the street into the classroom.

The material was new. The pressure wasn't.

Communication theory. Leadership models. Risk frameworks. Decision-making under uncertainty. I'd lived these things for years without calling them anything at all. Now they had names. Diagrams. Citations. It felt less like learning and more like decoding experiences I'd already survived.

In policing, you learn fast because mistakes are expensive. In the classroom, the students were quieter, but the discipline was the same. Show up prepared. Pay attention. Don't confuse confidence with certainty. Ask better questions than the person next to you.

Some nights, I left class carrying a backpack heavier than it needed to be, the smell of burnt coffee still on my breath. Mental fatigue hits differently. It's cleaner. Sharper. And strangely satisfying. I'd walk across campus under dim parking-lot lights, thinking about how familiar it felt to be tired for the right reasons.

I wasn't chasing reinvention.

I was stacking experience.

Just like rookies don't become officers overnight, I wasn't becoming anything new all at once. I was earning it—credit hour by credit hour, paper by paper, lesson by lesson. The same way the job teaches you: slowly, honestly, without shortcuts.

The bridge wasn't dramatic.

It didn't shake or sway.

It was solid, practical, and built to carry weight.

And this time, when I stepped forward, I wasn't guessing where it led.

I knew exactly why I was crossing it.

First Day in a Different Uniform

My first day in the corporate world didn't come with a siren. It came with a badge that opened a glass door and a lanyard that felt too light to be real.

I wore a dress shirt instead of a vest and leather shoes instead of boots. No radio weight on my shoulder. No extra magazines tugging at my belt.

As I walked down the hallway, I caught myself brushing my right hip without thinking—fingers searching for something that wasn't there. The space where my gun used to sit felt strangely hollow, like a missing word in a sentence my body still expected to finish. I let my hand fall, aware of it now, aware of how long instinct outlives necessity.

I walked into a building where nobody scanned hands, and nobody listened for a change in tone on dispatch. The quiet was different. It wasn't empty—it was controlled.

In the first meeting, tension arrived anyway.

A vendor dispute. A missed deliverable. A contract clause being interpreted three different ways by three different people. Voices rose, polite but sharp. The stakes were financial, reputational, and contractual—but the room felt familiar all the same.

I watched posture, cadence, and the way blame moved around the table looking for a home. I noticed who leaned forward when challenged and who leaned back when pressed. Who spoke to be heard and who spoke to be right. None of it required a badge to read. I didn't announce myself. I didn't need to.

I took one slow breath—the same breath Top taught me to take before stepping into a volatile room—and asked two questions I'd asked a hundred times on the street:

"What happened?"

"And what do we know for sure?"

The room settled.

Facts replaced speculation. Voices lowered. The story tightened into something that could be handled instead of argued over. What had felt personal a moment earlier became procedural. Solvable.

After the meeting, someone pulled me aside and asked how I stayed so calm.

I almost laughed.

Instead, I said, "Pressure is pressure. The trick is not letting it drive."

Later, walking back to my desk, I noticed my hand drift toward my hip again—lighter this time, more curious than reflexive. The habit was still there, but it no longer felt urgent. Just remembered.

That was when it landed for me.

The skills didn't die when the uniform came off.

They traveled.

What changed wasn't the work, but the setting. Instead of holding a line at two in the morning, I was holding clarity in daylight. Instead of separating chaos with commands, I was separating signal from noise with questions.

The uniform had changed.

The posture hadn't.

And for the first time, I understood that this wasn't leaving the job behind.

It was carrying it forward—without the weight, without the weapon, but with everything that actually mattered still intact.

What the Job Built

Even after I stepped into a new career, the streets didn't stop speaking to me.

Some habits don't leave—not for years, maybe not ever. I still scan mirrors on long drives. I still watch hands in passing cars. My knees remember the weight of the leather belt. My shoulders remember the pull of the vest. Sometimes, without thinking, my hand drifts toward the place my gun used to sit—an old reflex reaching for reassurance that isn't there anymore.

And every time I see a cruiser on the shoulder at night, blue lights washing the tree line, something in my chest tightens.

Not fear.

Not regret.

Recognition.

I remember the roadside conversations that never made reports. The smell of warm asphalt after sunset. The tick of an engine cooling while the radio waited. The quiet understanding that you were exactly where you were supposed to be, doing work that mattered whether anyone noticed or not.

I miss that sometimes—more than I admit. Purpose on the street is clean and immediate. You know why you're there. You know what matters. You know who has your back.

But I also know this: my family deserves the best of me, not the remainder. And the brotherhood that raised me doesn't require me to stay frozen in one role to honor it. Growth isn't betrayal. Moving forward isn't abandonment. It's a continuation.

So when I pass those blue lights now, I slow just enough—not to stare, but to pray. For the officer standing alone in the dark. For the driver trying to do better. For the night to end in stories, not scars.

Then I keep driving, carrying gratitude like a quiet badge no one can take.

These days, my mornings start with coffee instead of shoe polish. My calls arrive as calendar invites instead of tones. The adrenaline is different— steady, sustainable, the kind that sharpens thought instead of hijacking it.

And still, the job lives in me in all the right ways.

I lead meetings the way I once led scenes: by reading the room before the room reads me.

I handle conflict the way I handled domestics: by lowering the temperature before raising my voice.

I make decisions the same way I always have: slow enough to be deliberate, fast enough to matter.

The vocabulary changed.

The uniform changed.

The mission didn't.

Once, I ran toward the noise.

Now, I carry what it taught me forward—discipline, restraint, and a respect for the weight of consequences.

The job didn't harden me.

It clarified me.

And wherever this road leads next, I know this much is true:

This is my story, but it's also our story.

Epilogue—What Remains After the Noise

Some things stay with us not to weigh us down,
but to remind us who we became.

—Author's Reflection

The house rests in that quiet hour before dawn—the one that used to belong to the job.

Coffee cools on the counter. My son breathes steadily down the hall. The silence hums, not empty but alive, filled with what the noise once drowned out.

I used to think quiet meant absence.

Now I know it's a kind of arrival.

Outside, the streetlights fade against a warming sky. The same light that once shimmered across broken glass and rain-dark pavement now settles gently on the porch. I stand barefoot, mug in hand, listening to sounds I once believed were impossible for me—a single bird testing the morning, wind threading through the pines, and the low murmur of a road waking somewhere beyond the trees.

And every now and then, if I listen long enough, the silence rearranges itself into something familiar—a trace of radio static, a clipped voice carried on memory:

"Unit clear."

It isn't haunting.

It's a homecoming.

Because the night never really leaves you. It only changes tone.

I think of Top often—how he taught without speeches, how he steadied a world I didn't yet know how to face. His voice used to be instruction.

Now it's a memory. I hear it in the way people pause before speaking, in the way hands settle instead of clench, and in the quiet victories that never make a report.

Brotherhood was never the stories or the danger.

It was the frequency—the low, steady hum of people willing to show up in the dark and hold the line together.

That echo carries on. Not loudly. Reliably.

Maybe that's what legacy really is: not the noise we made, but the signal that remains after it fades.

The world still calls—just differently now. Through ordinary mornings. Through work done carefully. Through moments that ask for steadiness instead of speed.

Top once told me, "Your job isn't to chase peace—it's to make room for it."

I didn't understand then.

I do now.

So I breathe.

I let the quiet come all the way in.

Sometimes I still notice the instinct—the way my attention sharpens when blue light flickers on the horizon, the way my body remembers before my mind does. The feeling passes gently, like a song you no longer hear but still know by heart.

The rhythm is different now, but it's still there—in the hum of the refrigerator, in a house that wakes safely, in the ordinary mercy of morning.

Once, I ran toward the noise.

Now I live inside what it left behind.

Afterword

If you've made it this far, thank you. Books like this aren't written to explain a profession or to settle arguments. They're written to slow things down long enough to notice what often goes unseen.

The stories in these pages come from years spent in uniform, but they aren't meant only for those who wear one. They're about responsibility, restraint, and the quiet ways people learn to carry weight without letting it harden them. If any of this feels familiar, it's because these questions belong to more than one line of work—and more than one kind of life.

This book was written with deep respect for those who serve and for those who wait for them to come home. Every story is rooted in lived experience, but names, places, and identifying details have been changed or combined to protect privacy and honor the complexity of real lives. What matters most is not strict precision, but truth—the kind that reflects how people learn, falter, recover, and try again.

Much of this work happens quietly. It rarely announces itself. It shows up in small decisions, in patience under strain, and in moments when someone chooses steadiness over impulse. These are the parts that often go unseen, yet they shape who we become. This book exists to give shape to that quieter labor.

If these pages leave you with anything, I hope it's a little more patience for the unseen work people do every day. A little more curiosity before judgment. A little more room for grace—especially when the world feels loud and divided. And if you know someone who carries responsibility quietly, in uniform or out, I hope you'll check on them. Sit with them. Listen without trying to fix anything. Sometimes that is enough.

This book is not an argument or a defense. It is an attempt to name what often goes unspoken—the narrow space between public duty and private uncertainty, between strength and wear. If it resonates, that connection matters more than agreement.

To those who are still serving—sworn or civilian—please know that help exists and that reaching for it is a sign of strength, not weakness. This work can take more than it gives, and no one should have to carry that weight alone.

If you have lost someone—or if this work has taken something from you that cannot be replaced—please know this book was written with you in mind. It does not offer answers so much as recognition: a mirror for the courage, contradictions, and quiet humanity that shape a life of service.

Thank you for reading. And thank you for carrying these stories forward.

—Dr. Dondi M. Day

Support & Resources

If you or someone you love needs support, the following confidential resources are available:

- 988 Suicide & Crisis Lifeline
  Call or text 988 (U.S.)—available 24/7
- CopLine
  1-800-COPLINE (267-5463)
  Confidential peer support for active and retired law enforcement and their families
- Safe Call Now
  1-206-459-3020
  Confidential crisis support for first responders and family members
- Badge of Life
  badgeoflife.org
  Mental health education and support for law enforcement
- First Responder Support Network (FRSN)
  frsn.org
  Peer and clinical recovery programs

Speaking & Engagements

I didn't write *Ghosts, Smoke, and the Badge* to tell war stories.

I wrote it to explore what stays—long after the radio goes quiet.

From time to time, I make myself available to speak with departments, organizations, schools, faith groups, and community audiences about the themes woven throughout this book. These conversations are grounded in lived experience and centered on reflection, mentorship, resilience, and the quiet weight carried by those who serve.

Topics often include:

- Brotherhood and shared responsibility
- Leadership under pressure
- Coaching and mentoring through uncertainty
- Emotional control, resilience, and earned calm
- The unseen cost of service on individuals and families
- Integrity and decision-making when it matters most
- Building understanding between first responders and the communities they serve

These are not tactical presentations or political discussions. They are honest, human conversations—sometimes serious, sometimes reflective, often hopeful.

Formats may include:

- Keynote talks
- Small-group or facilitated discussions
- Q&A sessions
- Leadership or academy audiences
- Community or faith-based gatherings

If these themes resonate with your group, I welcome the opportunity to talk further.

Contact: dondi.day@hotmail.com

Thank you for the work you do—and for the conversations that matter.

—Dr. Dondi M. Day

Glossary

Badge – The metal insignia of office worn by law enforcement officers; in the memoir, it symbolizes both authority and moral weight, recurring as a metaphor for identity, reflection, and responsibility.

Bagpipes – Traditional Scottish instrument played during funerals and police memorials. Their sound is a recurring emblem of grief, honor, and brotherhood.

Basic Law Enforcement Training (BLET) – The state-mandated police academy program (North Carolina) certifying new officers through instruction in law, firearms, physical conditioning, and controlled response under stress.

Blue Lights – Emergency lights on a patrol car. Symbolically, they represent the enduring pull of the job, the instinctive reflex toward danger, and the emotional gravity that remains even after leaving the profession.

BOLO (Be On the Lookout) – A broadcast alert to officers to watch for a specific person, vehicle, or situation connected to a crime or safety concern.

Boredom Into Terror – A core motif describing the unpredictable shift from stillness to crisis that defines patrol work; reflects the mental discipline required to stay ready for sudden danger.

Brotherhood – The sense of loyalty and mutual understanding forged through hardship, humor, and shared trauma. A central emotional theme of the memoir.

Call/Call for Service – Any dispatched incident requiring police response, ranging from routine traffic stops to life-threatening emergencies.

Chicken Shack – A late-night diner serving as an informal decompression space for officers after difficult shifts—symbolizing camaraderie, release, and emotional repair.

Control – A core theme representing emotional regulation and composure under pressure; often associated with Top's teaching: "Slow down. Breathe. Think first."

Cruiser/Patrol Car – Police vehicle equipped with lights, siren, and radio communications; a recurring setting for reflection, tension, and transformation.

Dispatch / Dispatcher: The communications center that receives emergency calls and coordinates officers, fire, and EMS by radio.

Domestic (Call) – Short for domestic disturbance—one of the most dangerous and emotionally complex calls officers face, often involving family conflict or violence.

Dress Blues – Formal ceremonial uniform worn during funerals, memorials, and honor-guard duties.

Field Training Officer (FTO) – A senior officer responsible for training, evaluating, and mentoring new officers during their first months on patrol.

Funeral Detail / Honor Guard – Ceremonial police formation for fallen officers, including rifle volleys, flag folding, and the final radio sign-off ("10-42. Rest easy. We have the watch from here.").

Ghosts – Symbolic term for the emotional aftermath of traumatic calls—memories, regrets, and the lingering presence of the dead. Represents both psychological weight and the lessons carried forward.

Kevlar – Ballistic-resistant vest worn for protection. Mentioned in connection with high-risk scenes and the vulnerability of close-quarters encounters.

Last Call / 10-42 – A ceremonial final radio transmission given during an officer's funeral or last shift. Represents closure, honor, and the continuity of the brotherhood.

Magistrate – A judicial officer responsible for issuing warrants, setting bonds, and making initial determinations following arrests, depending on jurisdiction.

Off-Duty – Hours outside scheduled shifts when officers attempt to separate job from life. In the memoir, it also symbolizes the struggle to carry—or release—the emotional weight of the job.

Partner – The officer paired with another for patrol. Represents trust, vulnerability, and shared survival.

Patrol – Routine policing shifts that define the rhythm of an officer's life; the primary setting for much of the book.

Radio / 10-Codes – The constant auditory backdrop of police work, including coded language and tones that signal incidents. The sound of the radio becomes both a lifeline and muscle memory.

Roll Call – Pre-shift briefing where officers receive assignments, updates, and guidance before deployment.

Rookie/Probationary Officer – A new officer undergoing evaluation and training; the narrator's identity during early chapters.

Scene – Any location where officers respond to a call. The memoir also represents the emotional environment—the moment you step into and influence it.

Shift – A scheduled work period for patrol officers. The alternating nights and days shape both the rhythm and disorientation of the narrator's life.

Shift Meal – The improvised, often late-night meals officers share during or after tough calls; brief moments of human normalcy and camaraderie.

Solo Patrol – The point at which a rookie operates independently after field training—an emotional and professional milestone symbolizing both freedom and isolation.

Stop-Sticks – Tire-deflation device used to safely end vehicle pursuits.

The Diner – Another informal gathering spot like the Chicken Shack—portrayed as a place of brief human normalcy amid the job's intensity.

The Ghosts You Carry – A thematic phrase and chapter title referring to the accumulated emotional weight of trauma that officers bear long after incidents end.

The Job – Colloquial term for the culture, identity, and expectations of law enforcement. Represents both purpose and burden.

The Line / Holding the Line – A symbolic boundary between order and chaos, safety and danger. Reflects the officer's moral and physical duty.

The Noise – Recurring symbolic language representing chaos, adrenaline, danger, and inner turmoil.

The Quiet – Symbolic counterpart to "the noise," representing clarity, reflection, breath, and emotional steadiness.

Tones – Alert sounds broadcast over police radios to signal an urgent or high-priority call.

Top – The narrator's field training officer and guiding mentor; stoic, calm, and philosophically grounded in restraint and composure.

Traffic Stop – Routine vehicle stop for investigative or enforcement purposes. Illustrates both procedure and risk.

Threat Calculus – The rapid, often unconscious assessment of danger made by officers at every call; evolves in the memoir into emotional and moral calculus as the narrator matures.

Uniform – Both a literal and symbolic garment representing belonging, visibility, responsibility, and transformation of personal identity into a public role.

Welfare Check – A request for officers to check on someone's safety when there is concern they may be ill, missing, or in danger.

Understanding the Radio

For most people, a police radio sounds like static and numbers. To an officer, it's a living pulse—the voice that holds a shift together. Every call, every request for backup, and every clipped acknowledgment moves through that channel.

Ten-codes are shorthand—a compressed language built for speed and clarity. Instead of long sentences, first responders use standardized numerical signals ("10-4," "10-8," "10-33") to confirm status, request help, or flag emergencies. The meanings may vary slightly between agencies, but the rhythm rarely does: transmission, acknowledgment, silence, response.

That rhythm becomes instinct. You learn to hear stress before words fully form—the extra half-second before a reply, a unit number repeated once too often, a voice tightening just enough to change the air in the room. A pause between codes can say more than the code itself.

Dispatchers are the unseen anchor of every shift. They track units, relay information, and keep order inside the noise. Their calm tone—even when the room on the other end is anything but calm—sets the tempo for everyone listening. You might never meet the person behind that voice, but you trust them completely.

The radio becomes more than a tool. It's connection. It's the sound of a dozen lives moving through the same night, tied together by static, breath, and timing. The cadence settles into muscle memory—the hum between calls, the silence before something breaks, and the steady reassurance that someone else is listening.

Over time, that rhythm stays with you. Long after the radio is quiet, you still recognize its patterns—the way attention sharpens at certain tones, the way silence can feel full instead of empty. The language lingers, not as noise, but as awareness.

In that way, the radio is less about control than about connection. It teaches listening before reacting, steadiness before speed, and presence before action. It becomes a shared language of trust—one that holds people together in moments when clarity matters most.

Ten Codes

10-0—Use Caution

10-1—Signal Weak

10-2—Signal Good

10-3—Stop Transmitting

10-4—Affirmative

10-5—Relay (to)

10-6—Busy

10-7—Out-of-Service

10-8—In-Service

10-9—Say Again/Repeat

10-10—Negative

10-11—(On Duty / employee number slot)

10-12—Stand By (Stop)

10-13—Existing Conditions

10-14—Message / Information

10-15—Message Delivered

10-16—Reply to Message

10-17—En Route

10-18—Urgent / Quickly

10-19—In Contact

10-20—Location

10-21—Call ___ by phone

10-22—Disregard

10-23—Arrived at Scene

10-24—Assignment Completed

10-25—Report To/Meet

10-26—Estimated Arrival Time

10-27—License / Permit Info

10-28—Ownership Info (vehicle)

10-29—Records Check

10-30—Danger / Caution

10-31—Pick Up (prisoner / person)

10-32—Units Needed (specify)

10-33—Help Me Quick

10-34—Time

10-35—Valid Concealed Handgun Permit

10-36—Restraint Violation

10-40—Fight in Progress

10-41—Beginning Tour of Duty

10-42—Ending Tour of Duty

10-43—Chase

10-44—Riot

10-45—Bomb Threat

10-46—Bank Alarm

10-47—Complete Assignment Quickly

10-48—Detaining Subject, Expedite

10-49—Drag Racing

10-50—Collision—PD / PI / F (property damage / personal injury / fatal)

10-51—Wrecker Needed

10-52—Ambulance Needed

10-53—Road Blocked

10-54—Hit and Run (PD / PI / F)

10-55—Intoxicated Driver

10-56—Intoxicated Pedestrian

10-57—Request Chemical Analyst on Duty to Meet _____

10-58—Direct Traffic

10-59—Convoy or Escort

10-60—Investigate Suspicious Vehicle

10-61—Stopping Suspicious Vehicle

10-62—Burglary / Breaking & Entering

10-63—Investigate ___ at ___

10-64—Crime in Progress

10-65—Report of Armed Robbery

10-66—Notify Medical Examiner

10-67—Investigate Report of Death

10-68—Livestock on Highway

10-69—Advise Present Telephone Number

10-70—Improperly Parked Vehicle

10-71—Improper Use of Radio

10-72—Have Prisoner in Custody

10-73—Mental Subject

10-74—Prison or Jail Break

10-75—Records Indicate Wanted or Stolen

10-76—Report of Prowler

10-77—Assist Fire Department with Traffic

10-78—Report of Abandoned Vehicle

10-79—Report of Vehicle Fire

10-80—Report of Careless/ Reckless Driving

10-81—Report of High Speed

10-82—Report of Disabled Motorist

10-83—Report of Improper Registration

10-84—Report of Operator's License Violation

10-85—Report of Mini Bike/ Go-Cart Violation

10-86—Beginning Authorized Travel

10-87—Ending Authorized Travel

10-88—Unlawful Use of Mobile Device While Operating Vehicle

10-90—Rest Area/Welcome
    Center Check

10-91—CMV (Commercial
    Motor Vehicle) Inspection

10-92—School Safety Check
    at ___ School

10-99—Stolen

Reading Military Time

All times in this book are shown in military (24-hour) format, the standard used in law enforcement and emergency communications.

Standard Time	Military Time
Midnight	00:00
1:00 AM	01:00
2:00 AM	02:00
3:00 AM	03:00
4:00 AM	04:00
5:00 AM	05:00
6:00 AM	06:00
7:00 AM	07:00
8:00 AM	08:00
9:00 AM	09:00
10:00 AM	10:00
11:00 AM	11:00
Noon	12:00
1:00 PM	13:00
2:00 PM	14:00
3:00 PM	15:00
4:00 PM	16:00
5:00 PM	17:00
6:00 PM	18:00
7:00 PM	19:00
8:00 PM	20:00
9:00 PM	21:00
10:00 PM	22:00
11:00 PM	23:00

Acknowledgments

This book was shaped by the generosity, honesty, and discernment of many people who gave their time, insight, and trust throughout its development. From early readers who challenged structure and clarity to fellow officers, magistrates, dispatchers, and first responders who helped ensure accuracy and integrity, each of you strengthened this work in ways both seen and unseen. Your willingness to engage thoughtfully with these pages helped me remain faithful to the quiet weight and responsibility of the profession this book reflects.

With deep gratitude to Dan Willis—retired police captain, author, and teacher—whose generosity, wisdom, and steady voice helped set the tone for this book in ways I will always carry.

With sincere thanks to the following individuals, who offered early readings, perspective, and encouragement:

Steven Barzal, Senior Chief Petty Officer, U.S. Navy (Ret.)—friend and early reader

Michael Barzal—friend and early reader

Edward Blomgren, Sergeant, CID Major Crimes, Wake County Sheriff's Office (Ret.)—friend and early reader

Christina Campo—friend and early reader

Brad Creedon, Colonel—friend and early reader

Darrin Day, Captain (Ret.), Fairfax County Police Department—brother, mentor, and early reader

Donald Duncan, City Manager—longtime friend and early reader

Greg Percy, Chief of Police—early reader who generously reviewed the manuscript

Cesar Gonzalez Pelo, Captain—friend and early reader

Butch Wilkerson—friend and early reader

To those whose names are not listed here but whose conversations, examples, and quiet guidance shaped these pages: your influence is present throughout this work.

About the Author

Dr. Dondi M. Day spent more than twenty years in law enforcement, serving in small towns along North Carolina's coast and lower Piedmont, where boredom could turn into terror without warning and calm was learned the hard way. A graduate of the Basic Law Enforcement Training program at Carteret Community College, he earned advanced law enforcement certification and an Associate in Applied Science in Criminal Justice, grounding his career in both lived experience and disciplined preparation.

Over the years, he learned that the job was never just about calls cleared or arrests made. It was about judgment under pressure, restraint in chaos, and the quiet brotherhood formed among those who show up when others cannot. Those lessons—taught by mentors, mistakes, and long nights—shaped not only how he worked, but who he became.

After leaving law enforcement, Dr. Day transitioned into the private sector, where he built a second career focused on risk, leadership, and accountability. He currently serves as Vice President of Risk Management for a national energy services organization, overseeing contracts, safety, quality, and enterprise risk on complex, high-stakes projects. While the setting changed—from dark roads to boardrooms—the work remained familiar: reading situations clearly, making disciplined decisions, and holding steady when pressure rises.

Dr. Day holds a Doctor of Business Administration in Leadership from Liberty University, where his research examined how organizational culture shapes resilience and performance. He also earned a Master of Science in Administration from Central Michigan University and a Bachelor of Science in Business Administration from the University of Mount Olive.

A writer drawn to questions of duty, identity, and moral weight, Dr. Day brings a reflective, human lens to life inside—and beyond—the badge. *Ghosts, Smoke, and the Badge*: A Memoir of Brotherhood, Fear, and the Weight of Duty traces his journey from coastal Carolina nights to a life shaped by what the job leaves behind: steadiness, humility, and a commitment to serve with integrity.

He lives with his family in coastal North Carolina, carrying forward the lessons of the street into work, fatherhood, and the quiet spaces where meaning continues to take shape.

www.ingramcontent.com/pod-product-compliance
Lightning Source LLC
Chambersburg PA
CBHW071147130626

46553CB00004B/1565